03|

Wishing WELL

Wishing WELL

Empowering Your Hopes and Dreams

PATRICIA TELESCO

THE CROSSING PRESS
FREEDOM, CALIFORNIA

Copyright © 1997 by Patricia Telesco
Cover and Interior design by Victoria May
Set in Onyx, Janson Text, and Stone Sans
Printed in the U.S.A.

For information on bulk purchases or group discounts for this and other Crossing Press titles, please contact our Special Sales Manager at 800-777-1048.

Visit our Website on the Internet at: www.crossingpress.com

Library of Congress Cataloging-in-Publication Data
Telesco, Patricia, 1960-
    Wishing well, empowering your hopes and dreams / by Patricia Telesco.
        p.   cm.
    Includes bibliographical references.
    ISBN 0-89594-870-2 (pbk.)
    1. Magic.   2. Wishes.   I. Title.
BF1621.T45 1997
133.4'3--dc21   97-25971
                                                                                     CIP

Dedicated to:
Dreamers and believers everywhere
who gather up the starlight
hold it close to their hearts
and make wishes come true.

Acknowledgments

This book has truly been a community effort. I was amazed and very touched by the numbers of individuals who wrote with interesting wish lore. To mention a few by name and acknowledge the specific symbolic information they shared: Dorothy (birdseed, crochet, knots, tarot); Kalliope (bay leaf, Beltane, candles/yellow, incense, May Day, wax); Maeve (bread, candles/birthday, hair, horseshoes, needlework, oatmeal, star, tea); Megan (Yule); Starwood (cookie jar); and Taka (waking). Many thanks to each of you for gathering sparks that helped ignite the fires of wishcraft.

Specifically, thanks to Piers Anthony and Katherine Kurtz for taking the time to point out some useful resources. Despite their heavy writing responsibilities, these people have regularly answered my questions and letters. I have always appreciated this kindness and remember it when I answer my own mail.

My thanks also to:

—Darren F., with much appreciation for the expertise he shared regarding high magic and elemental creatures.

—Lisa Iris, Kalliope, Paul, and many other friends for networking my request via flyers, e-mail, mail, etc.

—David L., for his ever-faithful research assistance and generous lending of books from his personal library—with no due dates attached.

—and to *Fate* magazine for allowing portions of the article entitled "Wishcraft" to be reprinted.

Table of Contents

Introduction

Thoughts give birth to a creative force...thoughts create
a new heaven, a new firmament, a new source of energy
from which new arts flow.

—Zolar

Everyone has hopes and dreams. It is natural to want a better future, a future filled with contentment. A wish is the affirmation of that desire. It also can be an appeal to the universe for intervention.

Wishing on stars, tossing coins in a well, blowing out birthday candles—we've enjoyed these activities since our youth. We have all but forgotten the reasons for such actions, yet we engage in them just the same. Why are these seemingly illogical folkways still significant in our modern, sensible lives?

For example, many people wish on the first star that appears at night. In northern climes this is usually the North Star, which in ancient times was associated with Ishtar or Venus. To wish upon it was a prayer to the Goddess.

Philosophers supported this active form of prayer with their teachings. Plotinus, in *Enneads*, explained that magic and prayer work through sympathetic bonds that link everything to the celestial bodies in a harmonious network. Around the time of the birth of Christ, Ptolemy, a Greek astronomer, detailed in the *Tetrabiblos* the ways in which celestial objects influence life in complex ways. Aristotle later adapted Ptolemy's ideas, speaking of heavenly bodies as being responsible for promoting actions on Earth.

Do you walk around ladders, toss salt over your shoulder, or avoid black cats? Actions like these indicate a subconscious acceptance of old folk wisdom.

Each reenactment of a superstition gives it greater potency. Those we perform regularly become more powerful and assume the strength of rituals. Over our lifetimes and longer, the force behind these rituals will grow, but without direction. Wishcraft or intentional wishing provides that direction.

In wishing, a thought or verbal statement directs the energy accumulated by believing in a superstition, thus giving it a goal. The result is a potent combination of belief and ritual that can manifest itself in truly remarkable ways.

Wishing in this way also gives our aspirations tangible expression. Wishes are very important to our psychological health; they give us something to strive for.

When we cannot see exactly what steps are necessary to achieve our goals, wishing helps fill the gap. It gives us tools to understand the more universal meanings in our lives by revealing the symbols, wit, and wisdom of our ancestors. We can phrase our wishes in a contemporary fashion and direct our energy more specifically and more successfully.

In wishcraft, our innermost longings find expression and fulfillment. All magic has a will-driven mechanism, but wishing is also driven by hope. The first step to successful wishing is a correct understanding of our own desires. It is in our own hearts that we must begin.

Confidence and self-assurance are also important. If we conclude that a goal is unattainable, or too foolish, we renounce the power of wishing. For wishing to revolutionize our lives, we have to believe that our hopes are worthwhile and can be achieved. We also have to believe that personal aspirations are important and worthy of manifestation.

Therefore, we have to learn to trust ourselves and dare to dream in order to be effective in wishing. Our nature is a divine one, filled with creativity and talent just waiting to be tapped. Wishing can open those floodgates and help make our reality exactly what we want it to be.

When one looks at the world, the potential for wonders is everywhere. Plant a seed in the ground and watch it grow. That seed never questions its ability to sprout. The power is already within, waiting. The same notion holds true for your wishes. With the proper foundation and watering, wishcraft can transform the most mundane existence into a blossoming garden.

In these pages, I offer you a challenge. Ask yourself what you day-dream about. What would make you truly content spiritually and emotionally? Wishing can help you find what you really need. The minute you believe you have the power to change your life—you can!

Don't be afraid to wish. Dare to grasp for that tiny glint of starlight ... and may your wishes come true!

PART ONE

Manifesting Your Wishes

When you wish upon a star
makes no difference who you are
anything your heart desires
will come to you.

—*Jiminy Cricket in Walt Disney's* Pinocchio

The Fundamentals

*"Our wishes are the true touchstone of our estate; such
as we wish to be, we are."*

—Bishop Hall

Adults and children from all walks of life practice wishing. If you should ask them if they were casting a kind of spell, I suspect their answer would be no. For most people, wishing is simply a superstition that they engage in "just in case."

We treat wishing as a mini-ritual through repetition under specific circumstances. Give form and direction to that ritual, and it releases energy so that you can achieve your goals. While every wish may not be answered exactly as anticipated, positive efforts toward change will inevitably yield positive results.

This aspect of wishing is not magical at all. It is, rather, a way of thinking and "be-ing," of consciously originating the desired results. Instead of waiting for things to happen, we *make* them happen through positive efforts.

The application that follows will help you become more aware of opportunity and your innate ability to create openings through a combination of magic and fortitude.

APPLICATION 1

Decide on one wish you feel could reasonably be achieved within a month. For this exercise, make the wish as concrete as possible, and one that you can follow up on a mundane level. State your wish to the Universe on the first day of the month, and at the same time make a small token that represents the wish. For example, if you are wishing for money, carry a silver coin blessed by the waxing moon and wrapped with a dollar bill in your pocket.

Each day for the entire month, repeat your wish out loud three times. Besides this, make daily efforts to try to manifest that goal. In the aforementioned example, you might review the want ads or rework your budget. Keep hope and focus in your heart. By the end of the month, you should begin to see results from your magical energy and efforts. What happens then is that the daily voiced wish sends out energy to begin opening doors. It also sets up a resonance for success in and around your life. By going out and making efforts, you accept that success and become the key component to making your wish come true.

On a more metaphysical level this equates to being prepared, centered, and aware. Since like attracts like, the energy that returns to the active seeker in Application One is much *more positive*, and more suited to the wish they extended. As you go through this book, please bear this idea in mind.

It should be noted that the rational, practical mind also has a meaningful role in wishcraft. Your logical mind sorts wishes into categories and determines which should be attended to first. Add a little elbow grease, history, and creativity to this foundation and you're ready to begin!

Wishing in folklore and history

Old wives' tales, legends, and myths all have roles in the tradition of wishing. For convenience, I will gather these factors under the banner of folklore. By definition, folklore is a body of creative ideas about the supernatural, wisdom, beauty, ethics, and of course, wishing. Most authorities regard it as an oral tradition that develops among groups of people sharing common circumstances and experiences (see *Journal of American Folklore* in the bibliography).

The origins of folk beliefs clouded over time. It is a mystery why some folklore repeatedly finds expression in vastly different settings. For example, the flood myth appears in many cultures, among them the African, Incan, and Oceanic.

One theory is that there is a psychic unity to humankind, a condition that psychologist Carl Jung called the collective unconscious. This psychic unity is like a huge pool that anyone can drink from. When several people go to the pool simultaneously, they receive the same basic ideas; only the expression of that notion in society varies (see Dundes in the bibliography). Each cultural group finds ways to integrate these concepts into their society, and some of the ideas become traditions that are passed down through the centuries, slowly transforming into folklore, superstition, and ritual.

Changes in customs frequently mirror transitions in society. For example, today we may knock on wood as an affirmation of good fortune. Our ancestors may have knocked on wood to encourage luck, while our earliest progenitors worshipped the living spirit of the tree and didn't rap on it at all.

It is highly unlikely that the contemporary wood-knocker is knocking as an act of worship, but that does not diminish the importance of the gesture. Over time the veneration of trees has faded, but the fortunate energy associated with them remains, preserved by folklore. This preserved knowledge is used in wishcraft. Someone wishing for luck, for example, might use wood chips as an ingredient in lucky incense, or a wooden wand as a focus for a spell.

APPLICATION 2

In a small notebook, write down a list of five superstitions that you follow or that you see others following. Then look up the central object of the superstition in this book or another book of folklore to try and find its ancient roots. Once you have discovered information on one or two of the superstitions, ask yourself the following questions:

- Has the custom changed from its original form and/or meaning?
- If it has changed, was it due to changes in societal or cultural outlook?
- Can you see the progression the superstition took to get to its present form, and why?
- How can you adapt this tradition for your personal wishing?

Later, this type of exploration will prove very useful in designing meaningful wish spells, and also in improving your overall understanding of the ever-evolving human state.

In spellcraft, it is always better to understand why the components are being used. If something doesn't make sense in a magical procedure, it probably won't be effective. For example, the Norse runes were a magical alphabet that symbolically represented their hopes and dreams, as well as being a functional written language. The runes were under the dominion of Odin, the master of magical formulas and the god of wisdom and seership. Consequently, certain runes might be considered in your wishcraft to bring foresight and sagacity.

From this example, one can see that the form of wishes is always evolving. Future generations may pattern their own traditions on your inventive efforts today.

If information can be drawn from the psychic reservoir, then it seems equally feasible that information can be returned to it. Humanity has already gone to the water and received the concept of wishing. So, the next step is to convey our personal message of need (the wish) back into the pool, making a wave that is driven by magic. Somewhere in this reservoir of knowledge and energy, an answer to our wish will be found.

Wishcraft uses the familiarity of folklore as a mental advantage and part of this driving force. Folkloric actions are intrinsic to some aspects of our behavior and can be helpful to metaphysical efforts. A wish for luck might be enhanced by knocking on a wooden door, then opening that door. The motion of knocking announces your intentions to the Universe and your spirit. Then, opening the door welcomes that fortunate energy into your life!

To understand why folk wisdom complements wishing, remember that folklore, religion, and science danced closely together for eons. Only in recent years has the connection weakened. Fetishes, for example, are prepared using information gleaned from oral tradition. This qualifies the fetish as a kind of folklore. For certain tribal societies, fetishes are also intrinsic to religious observance. Beyond this, fetishes designed to aid the sick exhibit rudiments of scientific thinking (see Muller in the bibliography). For example, scientific research has uncovered many reliable curatives by studying early healing methods. To the untrained eye, the use of a toad to cure a patient with heart trouble seems silly. Yet modern physicians now know that toad skin produces a chemical similar to digitalis, used medicinally as a heart stimulant!

So, whether a family tradition is at the heart of your spell, or a custom from long ago, wishcraft begins restoring the connection between the esoteric and the mundane through practical magic and personal vision.

APPLICATION 3

Think back to childhood about superstitions that you either heard or followed regularly. Pick one that somehow reflects a wish you have right now. For example, in a wish for love, a daisy might become the focus or a wish for health might involve chicken soup.

Write down the day-to-day application for the superstition you've chosen, then begin to write words that freely associate with the tradition. For "daisy," a word association might be "pick—pluck—rhyme—throw—wind—loves me."

Review what you've written. This will be the foundation of your wish spell. For the daisy, one might pick it by sunrise (for hope), pluck each petal while reciting a rhymed incantation, and throw the petals to a southerly wind (for passion). Or, carry the daisy petals as a fetish/charm to draw love into your life!

Keep a notebook of all such personally devised wishes. You will want to use these again and again, making them feel like old, familiar friends, which is exactly what they are. You are effectively reclaiming this tradition for personal empowerment.

Not too long ago a child might have wished to travel the stars, and if someone appeared in a spacecraft, it would have been regarded as magical. In this respect, today's mysteries, folklore, and wishes may become tomorrow's science. Thus, we can anticipate science revealing what spiritual seekers and dreamers everywhere have always believed: everything is connected, everything has a purpose, and we have the power within to fundamentally change our reality. This is also the essence of wishing.

What to expect

Have you ever heard someone tell you to "be careful what you wish for, you just may get it"? This aphorism is crucial to successfully using this book. In *Sorcery*, Finley states that it is human nature to envision that our aspirations will be fulfilled in an idyllic form. How they really manifest themselves may be another story altogether.

Let's use love as an example. The images we get from the media and our own minds are mostly romantic, passionate, and filled with happy endings. For most people, however, life just isn't that perfect. It is unfair to expect our life mate to be flawless, and there is no such thing as "happily ever after". In this context, the outcome of wishing may seem disappointing at first. Also, every spell yields slightly different results depending on your mood, concentration, resolve, and the intrusion of everyday reality. The phone might ring, a dog might bark, or you might sneeze at the wrong moment. Such things can derail your train of thought.

Because of these limitations, it is important to be realistic with your expectations. Wishing isn't a cure-all for the bumps and bruises of life. It probably won't make you famous overnight or heap money on your doorstep. Rather, wishing puts a new fire under coals you may have set aside, forgotten, or given up on.

APPLICATION 4

Identify one hope, wish, or dream you have had that you regret not pursuing. Write down this wish in its most perfect, idealistic, romanticized form with all the bells and squeaks. Consider how a Hollywood movie would portray the "happily ever after" ending to your wish, and take your cue from that.

On another sheet of paper, list the practical steps you feel need to be taken to achieve your goal. Be as detailed and organized as possible. Below this, list the reasons you gave up on your dream in the first place.

On a third sheet, write down what you believe would be the realistic outcome of the wish, if pursued both magically and mundanely.

Review all this information, then ask yourself if this goal is still realistic, knowing the limitations you discerned.

I think you will find this exercise enlightening. The things we regret often stem from the more romantic, idealistic visions of our wishes rather than from the reality. Additionally, we may one day discover that what life gave us instead was much better and made us much happier. We don't always know what's best, but using a process like this helps us to see what is possible, probable, and what is actually not as great as it seemed.

I have always believed that for any form of magic to work well, we must remain active participants in the process of change. If, for example, you wish for a new job, you should also be earnestly updating your resume, reviewing advertisements, and interviewing so that the Universe can present the opportunity you wish for. Wishcraft provides the zeal and confidence you need to act on your hopes, and generates more energy for the mundane portion of the equation. As wishing works its magic in your heart, and confidence grows, success in all your endeavors follows naturally.

The will in wishing

The concept of personal will must be considered in any discussion of magic. No matter the path you follow, spells are will-driven mechanisms. They draw on universal energy and individual fortitude for expression.

Willpower is vital for mastering your craft. If you doubt its significance, just watch a stubborn child sometime. Single-minded determination frequently results in the child getting exactly what he or she wants. While most adults do not resort to such tactics, we can learn much from children's persistence. They refuse to give up, and believe wholeheartedly that their desire is worthy of your complete attention.

This kind of tenacity, when developed, greatly benefits spiritual endeavors. By being steadfast, you insist that the matter in question deserves serious notice from the Universe. Repeating the wish several times sends out waves of sympathetic energy to help it come true. Just like the proverbial message in a bottle—eventually the energy returns to shore of the psychic reservoir with a response.

A P P L I C A T I O N   5

Think of a wish that has a long-term goal, one you believe will take a year or more to manifest. On New Year's Day (or any day you deem appropriate, such as your birthday), make your wish in whatever form feels right. Also make a promise to yourself and the Universe to recite the wish daily for a year, and do everything in your power to help the wish along in the real world. Do not make this commitment lightly; you only cheat yourself by disregarding it.

Each time the wish spell is cast, focus strongly on your goal, and use your will power to direct the resulting energy. Also use that same tenacity to empower and guide your practical efforts. The results should be quite impressive.

After several months, you will find the wishing comes naturally, as do your support efforts. You will begin recognizing openings more readily because you are already focused on your goal. The positive attitude you display will affect everyone in and around the wish, including yourself. These good vibrations set up a daily resonance to help create the right time, place and opportunity for your wish to manifest itself. Make notes of the results in your journal.

Responsible magic

In the above exercise and in all of magic, it is your will that raises, directs, and manifests magical energy. Consequently, accountability for the wishes you render lies totally with you. This knowledge should inspire careful thought before performing any type of magic. Our daily actions have ramifications, some of which are obvious and some of which can only be imagined. Endeavors influencing the astral plane are no different.

All magic works within certain universal limits, coupled with other limits provided by the elements of our spells (verbiage, visualization, and so forth). What we don't know is the full impact this may have. For example, we might achieve a general wish for fertility by getting pregnant, having more creative energy, or seeing our garden grow abundantly!

For a moment, think of magic as a huge spider web with your spell in the middle. Time and space move out from this spot in an unending mesh. When your vision reaches its spiritual horizon, you can see no further; you've reached the web's border. From that instant forward, we must trust in the spell's construct for direction and completion. If no construct exists, then the Universe will take the most natural, unimpeded course toward manifestation, which may or may not produce what you envisioned.

One example of this comes from a recent lecture series. A young woman related a story about wishing to banish the negativity in her office. While on vacation, she cast a spell for that purpose, but it was very generalized. When she returned, she found many people out of the office, either sick or dealing with personal problems. She literally banished the people from the office, negativity and all, instead of producing just the positive energy!

Therefore, you can see that it is prudent to construct your wishcraft so that it *specifically* defines your goal(s).

APPLICATION 6

Write down a wish's goal answering all the "W's" — who, what, where, why, and when. Include all this information in the verbal or written form of the wish spell, or among its components in symbolic form. This process forces you to think seriously about the wish, what it means to you, and how it may affect others.

For example, you may wish to improve your relationship with your life partner. The "who" of this equation is you and your partner. "What" is the relationship itself. "Where" is within the heart, the traditional emotional center. "Why" is so that your life together may be joyful and fulfilling. "When" is probably as soon as possible, but relationships require time and effort, so the results probably won't be instantaneous.

Next, add any other components appropriate to your purpose. In this illustration, a visual aid that shows two halves of one heart uniting is quite a potent token, but be sure you have the right hearts! Write your names on the two halves and add a non-manipulative incantation that lets nature take its course. Bring the two halves together and attach them to each other in some way.

When casting the wish spell add a phrase that many witches use: "For the greatest good, and it harm none." The effect is very responsible, symmetrical spell-casting with good results.

Finally, keep the token safely stored near the hearth or stove of your home, as this was considered the "heart" of the home by the ancients. It is also a warm region that engenders warm feelings.

Word power for wishing

In *Words of Power* by Brian and Esther Crowley we read, "The use of sound for specific purposes is universal and historical." The power of language is something philosophers, artists, rulers, and students of the occult have all pondered. Many have successfully wielded word power to their benefit.

In ancient Japan the samurai warriors used the *kiai* or "shout of power." The action it described was exactly that, a great shout before entering battle. According to Lafcadio Hearn, in Japan a specific word or phrase directed the inner focus of the samurai, gave him greater strength, and startled opponents.

During the Middle Ages, *jongleurs*—itinerant minstrels—used language to arouse the emotions of their listeners. A talented singer or storyteller would net far more gold if her/his words reached people's hearts, not just their ears. The art of the troubadour was important to the integrity of oral tradition, which preserved local history through memory.

Where did these people, and others like them, get the idea that words were so potent? Reviewing the earliest stories of the gods uncovers a partial answer. In the *Book of Genesis*, God created the world by expressing words of command. The *New Testament* stated that the Word and the divine image were one and the same (*John 1:1*). In ancient Egypt, the god Ptah thought of all things, then uttered the words that manifested his visions (see Cavendish, 1977, in the bibliography). This type of creation myth is foundational to many cultures.

The power ascribed to divine words grew proportionally with each recital of the ancient stories. Sacred texts and languages became common among many great civilizations. The Egyptians even revered their hieroglyphics as the "speech of the gods."

This is very important to comprehending how and why word power works. Once we realize that part of the Great Spirit dwells within us, we also accept the inherent divinity of speech. Like the ancients, we can reclaim language as a great gift and learn to use its energy wisely.

In his *Encyclopedia of Ancient and Forbidden Knowledge* Zolar said, "Assuredly: the power to make and change the mind dwells within, for the mind is only an instrument in the hands of the self...but we must realize this and not just believe it." This statement highlights two important aspects of word power. First, it shows that our ability for transformation is internal. Second, we must accept this ability as fact, not just as a possibility. When these two components combine within our minds, something truly extraordinary is born: positive, empowering speech.

A P P L I C A T I O N   7

Sit in a comfortable position and think of a short phrase that describes your fulfilled wish—peaceful home, loving marriage, bills paid, etc. Close your eyes and breathe deeply, in through your nose and out through your mouth. As you do, visualize a bright white light pouring down upon you from above.

Within the light, see the words you have chosen sparkling with silvery power. These keep pouring into your mind and down toward your mouth until the energy must break free. As it does, shout or sing your wish to the winds and let magic have its way!

Think of a simple wish you have. For one week, each time you talk about that hope, speak positively and confidently about it. Instead of using phrases like "well, we can always hope," change your way of communicating so it affirms your wish. For example, answer a question about your wish with the words, "Yes, results are just around the corner." As these words are spoken, and that assurance and faith moves through the air, it changes the vibrations around a person to encourage success.

To cite a personal example, I was frustrated for about eighteen months with my inability to complete a manuscript to a publisher's satisfaction. I couldn't figure out what was wrong until I realized that I had gotten so frustrated that my words reflected defeat. When I changed the way I thought and spoke about that project, and trusted in its worthiness, a contract (from another publisher) came through within two weeks! Sometimes the Universe requires these types of transformations in our thinking. After all, if we don't have faith, why even try to work magic?

Each expression of constructive beliefs helps reinforce our sense of worth. This is one step toward becoming self-actualized and believing in our divine potential. Words take on a magical quality the minute we acknowledge that divine nature. As our faith grows, so do the flames that engender change. Wishing taps these spoken "fires" to make wishes come true.

When using the term "speech," however, I am not necessarily denoting spoken words. Thoughts, as electrical mechanisms, are just as important and powerful, and there are times when it is not socially acceptable to be reciting an affirmation or power shouting! Better still, when we stop thinking in negative or restrictive terms, our activities mirror that change, and we reclaim the capacity to work miracles.

14 steps to effective wishing

In the old days, when someone needed water they would take a bucket to the well. Wishing has something in common with both the bucket and the water. The bucket equates to your hands, mind, and heart gathering the supportive energy to make your wishes come true, as you have done in many of the exercises in this book. The water is the creative willpower you have within to facilitate manifestation. Neither the bucket nor the water will be much use, however, if you aren't willing to go to the well! That's where this section can help.

The following fourteen steps are meant to guide you in designing, casting, and releasing your wish towards its goal. As always, adapt these suggestions to your own path and vision for the most powerful and personally significant results.

1. Defining Your Goal

Think of yourself as an architect. The building you are designing is your life. You will need specific plans to lay it out just right. This is where defining your goal becomes exceedingly important.

For example, we all want to be happy. What will make *you* happy? The Universe will respond to a wish for joy, but its manifestation can be quite unexpected. To avoid having your intentions misconstrued, your wish should be constructed in terms as precise as a builder's blueprint.

APPLICATION 9

Breathe deeply for a few minutes, emptying your mind of everything but the issue central to your wish. Using a medium you are comfortable with—such as writing, painting, or singing—let your ideas flow freely, then review and edit them. Condense the entire outpouring into a few simple, positive images with strong emotional impact. Keeping these key images positive helps to avoid the influence of contrary energy. Here is a sample that uses writing:

> **Original outpouring:** I wish for the prosperity of my family. Not so much to be rich, but to give my children a better life. I'm tired of saying "no" all the time. It makes me sad and frustrated. I hate choosing between paying the bills and eating. I'm tired of life handing us lemons. I hate lemonade!

Key images:	Say yes to life!
	Prosperity, providence and joy!
	Happy, contented children.

Now determine the best way to utilize your resulting constructs in your wish magic. From Application Nine, for example, the first phrase might become an affirmation to recite upon rising each day. The second becomes a verbal component in spell work. The last becomes a part of a prayer. Each, in its own way, conveys the wish to the greater powers, but more importantly, clarifies the goal in your own mind, where magic really begins.

2. Choosing and preparing your symbols

Once you have fully defined your goal, consider how to best represent it with objects in magical terms. Your circumstances will often help determine this. Many objects have traditional associations that remain powerful. For example, a candle is the perfect symbol for wish magic cast on your birthday. Likewise, a wishbone is a good choice when wishing for a bountiful harvest, since it comes from a creature that supplies nourishment. Coins are excellent choices for wishes relating to luck, wealth, and safe travel.

To facilitate your selection process, refer to Part Two of this book for lists of objects, plants, animals, and minerals, and their traditional symbology.

A P P L I C A T I O N 1 0

Think of one wish. What are the very first symbols that come to mind in relation to your wish? If you find yourself drawing a blank, check dream dictionaries for some ideas. Make a list of these symbols. Which are readily available to you? How do you want to put the components together—into an incense, a portable charm, a visual spell? Once you've answered these questions, you're ready to begin.

3. Cleansing and consecrating your symbols

After reviewing your list of items and gathering those readily available to you, take a moment to cleanse, bless and consecrate them. This will relieve them of any accumulated energy, encourage divine favor, and dedicate them for their specific function.

Cleansing can be accomplished in several ways, the simplest of which is immersing the symbol in spring water or smoke. The spring water can also be enhanced with a little lemon juice. The smoke should be generated from cleansing herbs like clove, pine, or cedar, ignited in an incense burner or fire. You can also place the objects in rich soil or sea salt (as long as they won't be harmed). The soil represents growing, fertile energy, and it absorbs impurities naturally. Salt is a purgative.

Consecration involves calling on a god/dess image or Universal Power to bless your symbols. I like to use a short prayer, including a brief description of intended use. During this prayer, I lift each component to the sky. To complete a writing project, for example, I might hold a favorite pen upwards and say, *"Oghma, Vach, heed my prayer! Bless this instrument of creativity that only words filled with truth and light may flow. Guide my hand for this sacred task. So be it."* In this prayer I've asked for help from the Irish god of writing, Oghma, and the Hindu goddess of magical discourse and mantras, Vach (for more information on gods and goddesses see step 6).

Following this procedure, return each symbol to the altar or work space until you cast your spell.

4. Using your symbols in ritual

After proper preparation, exactly how you use each token in your spell is up to you. To maintain congruity, however, whatever you do to the token in your sacred space should mimic your purpose. In an earlier example of a wish for love, two paper hearts became the central representation of the wish. During the spell, these are moved closer together or loosely bound with a purple thread (for romance). This way, the visual impact of the wish magic generates additional sympathy.

Here are just a few transformable objects and the themes to which they might be applied:

Object	Themes
Ice	Melting a hard heart; freezing negativity within; carving the image of what you wish to rid and letting it melt.
Rope	Networking, Connections, Bindings
Paper	Release your wish to heaven with an origami image of it, which is burned.
Bread dough	Increase (cast your spell while baking the loaf, adding compatible herbs).
Candy	Internalizing joy, sweetness, and positive attributes.
Rubber band	Expansion or growth within specific limits.

Your chosen components also serve a secondary purpose. They provide a focus for your mind and spirit. Burn a specially prepared incense, play some thematic music, dance, sing or do whatever else feels right to you. Remember that these extra embellishments should help settle your thoughts and induce a meditative state. This enhanced mental receptivity allows energy to flow more freely and accurately.

5. Timing

When is the best time to make a wish? Anytime can be the "right" time for magic if you have the desire, inner resolution, and proper attitude. But there are traditionally favorable times. If you want to provide your spell with growing power, cast it during a waxing moon. This helps with manifestation. Customarily, evening is a great time, because stars are so strongly associated with making wishes. Other favorable times are during a blue moon, on Wednesdays, when the moon is in the sign of Virgo or Pisces, when rainbows are visible, and during the month of April. This is by no means a complete list. Additionally, there are wishes that do not fit these scenarios at all.

For example, when requesting that a negative habit like procrastination or distractibility be removed from your life, daylight hours and waning moons are more fitting. Daylight emphasizes the logical, cognizant mind. The decreasing moon is symbolic of departure. The intention of your wish best determines whether a specific timing is called for. But the best general guideline is to follow your gut instinct.

APPLICATION 11

If you want to delay wishing until a specific, auspicious time, consider the following:

- Are there any dates or times that you strongly associate with the theme of your wish? Your birth date enhances magic for new beginnings and longevity. Your wedding anniversary is an excellent date to direct wishcraft for renewed romance and lasting love.

- Are there specific seasons that might accent your wish? For example, conception wishes gain energy in spring, the season of birth and fertility.

- Are there any holidays that seem related? New Year's is a perfect time for resolution and personal change. Yule inspires the spirit of kinship. The most positive memory or feeling you associate with a holiday will help to determine its significance to your wish.

- Are there any moon phases or astrological signs that have sympathetic energy to the goals of your wish?

- Can your wish wait, or is immediacy important? It might be best to act on a wish right away, while you have the willpower to support it.

Make a list of preferred times for your wish spells, by theme, in your journal for future reference.

Early mages believed that daily, seasonal, and celestial influences could help ensure the potency of a spell. Our use of astrology today comes from that tradition. Refer to a good astrological calendar for specific advice, as influences change from year to year due to lunar, planetary, and solar cycles. Below is a brief chart of some of the more common correspondences.

Timing	Themes
Dawn, Waxing Moon	Beginnings, hope, growing awareness
Noon	Banishing negativity, strength, courage, power, masculine traits
Dusk, Waning Moon	Endings, completion, the past
Night, New Moon	Rest, solitude, waiting
Full Moon	Fertility, maturity, harvest, the feminine aspect, instincts
New Year's	Resolution, transformation
Spring	Awakening, renewed energy and hope
Summer	Abundance, socialization, energy
Fall	Harvest, natural bounty, frugality
Winter	Halted movement, conservation
Birthday	Renewal, change, acceptance, resolve, health, blessings
Wedding Anniversary	Love, devotion, commitment, promise

6. Choosing divine guidance

In my example in the earlier section about consecrating symbols, I called upon two deities strongly associated with writing. Using a specific god or goddess in your spell can be helpful. As with choosing components, deciding among the many faces of the Great Spirit makes you think more clearly about your wish.

Do you want to call on a god/dess from your personal belief system? Do you want the aid of a deity traditionally associated with your goal? Or, would you prefer just to ask for a general blessing? All three of these approaches can be perfectly fitting. What matters most is finding something that feels right and makes sense to you.

It is always important, however, to have a good understanding of any deity you call upon. For example, while Kali is a goddess of purification, her methods are harsh, fast, and unforgiving. She may not be the best choice for a cleansing wish or prayer. And make sure you pronounce the god/dess's name correctly, have fitting incense or altar decorations, and honor her/him with a proper welcome.

For many years I felt uncomfortable with praying because it reminded me of church. When I began to equate prayer with chanting or a mantra, the process finally became more "user friendly" to me. No matter what your approach, find a personally meaningful way to draw universal energies into your sacred space to whisper your wish directly to them.

There are several books that detail the gods and goddesses of the world. These also give you important information on appropriate ways to invite these powerful, sacred forces into your magical space. I recommend *Ancient Shining Ones* by D. J. Conway, and *The Witches' God* and *The Witches' Goddess* by Janet and Stewart Farrar. A listing of wishing deities is also included in Part Two of this book.

7. Adding word power

Find or prepare appropriate invocations, incantations, and chants. These will change depending on your wish and the god/dess you intend to invoke. If writing isn't your strong suit, browse a few volumes of poetry, some favorite magical texts, or other literary sources for ideas. Often the perfect item just pops into your hands. If not, look for something close, then make appropriate modifications.

Don't overlook the key phrases that highlight your goal. Using the example from Application 9 (p. 27), a chant for abundance becomes:

"Say yes to life, and blessed be
today I claim prosperity!"

Embellishments can be added, like sprinkling rice in a circle clock-wise as your chanting grows louder. Rice is a symbol of providence, moving clockwise draws positive energy, and chanting builds power.

APPLICATION 12

This application requires about 45 minutes to an hour. Take out five sheets of paper. At the top of each of the five sheets write one of the following five words respectively: LOVE, PEACE, JOY, HEALTH, WEALTH. Underneath each word, write down synonyms, terms that you personally associate with it, as well as words that rhyme with any of these. A sample word list for peace might look something like:

Rhymes	Synonyms	Rhymes for Synonym
Cease	Tranquil	Hill, Sill, Fill
Least	Calm	Balm, Palm, Psalm
Feast	Accord	Poured, Stored
Keys	Rest	Best, Zest, Test

These associated words can then become part of a rhyming invocation, prayer, incantation, or affirmation. For example:

> Let peace fall soft, at my window sill
> and all within be tranquil
> Accord, here poured
> Peace be restored.

You don't have to write award-winning poetry to be effective. What's most important is that the final phrases are comfortable for you and sincerely convey your wish. Embellishments for this spell may include a warm, cozy blanket laid upon the inner window sill.

8. Preparing the sacred space

In the interest of clean, controlled energy, having a specially pre-pared area for wishing is always a good idea. It provides a purified area, free from psychic clutter, within which you can feel totally at home. It creates a barrier between you and any unwanted influences. It concentrates your power until you feel completely ready to release and direct it. Casting a circle invites each elemental guardian—Earth, Air, Fire, Water—into your sacred space, forming a complete sphere of spiritual energy around, above and below you.

The Spiral Dance by Starhawk, and *To Ride a Silver Broomstick* by Silver RavenWolf are two excellent guides with specific suggestions for creating a sacred space.

A P P L I C A T I O N   1 3

It is fairly easy to create an appropriate space for your wish magic. Find four objects that can become symbols of the four elements in your sacred space. For example, a small vessel filled with water might represent water, a candle fire, a fan air, and a crystal earth. Take a moment to cleanse and bless these objects. Then place them in a circle at the points of the compass at which their elements are associated: north and earth, south and fire, east and air, west and water. Fashion a simple altar or work-space using a small table or similar object that has special mean-ing to you. On this altar you will place objects or tokens that have significance in the spell you cast.

9. Creating a meditative state

A sacred space within your heart and mind is just as important to wishing as your physical space. Using simple methods like deep rhythmic breathing, chanting, and visualization, you can achieve a meditative state and create an internal sacred space. The goal is to focus your mind and spirit to the task ahead, and to rid yourself of lingering mundane thoughts that might derail your wish magic.

If you don't already incorporate some type of meditation into your daily routine, you should consider doing so. It is an effective aid to creating the inner focus and resolve necessary for success in any endeavor.

Start by finding a comfortable position that you can stay in, undisturbed, for twenty minutes or so. Breathe deeply and begin to release the tension from every part of your body. Think about your wish. Visualize it. Speak the wish out loud if it helps. Let the image or sound of the wish capture your entire attention. Let it consume you until your body feels as if it is vibrating with that energy. As you cast your wish spell, use this power as a driving force for manifestation.

10. Using senses to strengthen wishing

The most important factors for success in wishing are concentration, will, and confidence. But each one of your senses has the potential to further clarify your goal, heighten awareness, and add power to your wish.

Sight aids in visualizing your aims. Smell is more primal, providing stronger emotional and instinctual focus. Touch improves your physical understanding of intentions. Taste helps you internalize your goal. Hearing helps with deepening meditative states and directional guidance.

If you're working to improve a relationship, for example, here are some items you might use to engage your senses:

Sight: A photograph or personal items displayed on the altar in plain view.

Taste: Favorite foods or beverages, especially offerings that also reflect the goal. (Strawberries, for example, are love fruits.)

Smell: Cologne or perfume associated with the other person used as part of an incense.

Hearing: Soft, romantic music. Chants, songs, incantations and invocations whose words strongly reflect your goal.

Touch: Warm, cozy clothing, just as you wish the relationship to be!

How you incorporate each sense into your wishcraft is personal. If it is impossible to utilize all of them, focus on the sense or senses that you respond to most strongly.

APPLICATION 15

To find out which senses you understand and respond to most intimately, select three hand-size objects and put them on a table. Sit down in front of these, and examine them with your eyes. Note as many details as you can, and write your observations down. Next, close your eyes and feel the items with your hands, again noting your impressions. Follow in kind by smelling them, tasting them, and listening to them. Which of your five senses gave you the strongest feedback? Which two? Which three?

11. Casting the wish spell

Once you've gathered your components, composed your incantation, chosen an appropriate time, and prepared your sacred space, you are ready to cast your spell.

Enter the sacred space mindful of your purpose, visualizing it in detail. Take a deep breath, center yourself, and begin to visualize strands of white light connecting the tokens together in a clockwise circle. Let this light also connect you with the tokens until a fine web of energy forms around, above, and below you. At this point, begin your wish spell. Use the chosen components to give focus to your spell. Build the energy through word and deed. Add chanting, singing, music, dance, meditation, or anything else that focuses more energy toward your wish. Take your time, and continue until you feel confident that the power has reached a pinnacle.

12. Releasing the magic

For all your efforts, magic will do little good if you don't release it. It's like a bow and arrow. You can pull back the bowstring with determination and aim the arrow perfectly, but until you release it, you haven't shot the arrow.

To free the energy you've raised, use whatever combination of visualization, action or sound that seems appropriate, depending on your situation. Visualize the energy web that surrounds you opening up to let the spell out. Move your hands upward, or something similar, to nudge it on its way. Speak strong, singular words to direct it.

In reviewing the methods of wishing presented here, you will notice a recurrence of certain procedures used to send magic on its way. You may use the procedure given, or another of your choosing. However it is a good idea to know ahead of time which approach you will use in the sacred space. Your choices include:

- Burying the object after the wish has been inscribed upon it, or after visualization. Here the wish is likened to a seed, lovingly placed in the ground to grow.

- Releasing the symbol of your desire—such as herbs or ashes—to the wind or in water. Both denote movement to convey the energy toward your goal. Whenever you use this technique, please take extra care that your symbol is biodegradable and not harmful to animals.

- Carrying a charm, emblem or other token with you for a period of time. This attracts corresponding energy and keeps the power of your wish close to you. Keep it on the receiving side of your body (whichever hand you use to accept a gift) or near your heart for best results. If this is not possible, put the token where it will be seen regularly, like on a mirror or the dash of your car.

- Presenting an item or items to someone to extend a special wish to them. This is commonly seen at weddings where a couple is showered with rice so they may never want, or given a bundle of hazelnuts for fertility. In this instance wishcraft blossoms outward, showing consideration and kindness toward the important people in our lives.

Once released, remember to continue guiding the wish until it reaches your spiritual horizon. Lastly, close your sacred space by dissolving the surrounding web of energy, disconnecting yourself from the tokens, then the tokens from each other in a counter-clockwise direction. Dismiss and thank your guardians, let the candles burn out, and say a final prayer or whatever suits the moment.

Then trust in yourself, your magic, and the Divine to direct the wish to its destination.

13. Repeating the wish

Repetition may not be necessary for your spell. But you may feel more empowered and confident if you repeat it regularly until it manifests. It is *your* will at work here, and *how* it works best is up to you.

APPLICATION 16 :

One simple way to reinforce your wish, if you choose to, is with incantation. Every time your wish comes to mind, repeat the chant you developed for your spell seven times (the number of completion), visualizing the manifestation of your goal. This does not require any planning, special timing or preparation, which is perfect if you have a hectic schedule. Each reiteration provides the original magic with an extra boost and focuses your thoughts again toward your goal. It also gives you something positive to do when you're feeling anxious or impatient.

14. Follow-up

Now begin honest, tangible efforts to help manifest your wish. Get to work on that résumé. Plan a retreat for you and your significant other. Do whatever is appropriate to lend substance to your goal. Like any transformational journey, wishing starts with one, brave step toward visualizing your dreams. Then comes the hard, day-to-day work. They complement each other in the realization of your goal.

*True Religion shows its influence in
every part of our conduct;
it is like the sap of a living tree
which penetrates the most distant of boughs.*

—*William Penn*

Strengthening Your Wish Power

Choose out a gift from seas, earth or skies, for open to your wish all nature lies.

—Addison

Once you've put the fundamentals of wishcraft into practice, it may prove necessary to focus and strengthen your spell work with greater definition. The following techniques will help modify your wishing so it flows more smoothly in your life. They are slightly more intricate than previous techniques, and are designed to improve your magical proficiency. Simple forms of wishing function perfectly well, and just like the proverbial soup pot, having too many ingredients can spoil an otherwise wonderful blend. Therefore, carefully add these techniques to your methods, testing them as you go. Once you're happy with the results, stop and take note. You can return again and again to these methods, devised by your own hands, heart and path.

Living your wishes

A Japanese proverb says, "You start digging the well when you are thirsty." More than likely, you have begun to explore wish magic because you have a need. What happens, though, when you have finished your spell? Do you forget about it and go on with your routine? Absolutely not!

Living a magical reality means doing normal things in a not-so-normal way. Wishcraft is a way of thinking, doing, *and* being. It denotes creation and action. Reinforcing your magic by word and deed produces the most dramatic results. While this may seem superficially obvious, many people overlook it. They fantasize about their desires, but fail to take the leap of faith necessary to manifest them. This self-trust, this belief in the inevitability of your wish's fulfillment finds its expression in your subsequent actions.

APPLICATION 17

Think of a relatively simple wish and come up with five viable, everyday reinforcements for it. Create your wish spell for this goal, following the guidelines given in the previous chapter. After your spell has been cast and released, commit yourself to following it up with each of the five reinforcements as often as possible for at least one week. Carefully note the results.

To provide a personal illustration, I once wished to get good leads for selling my home-made products. The components for my spell included the local Yellow Pages, a list of personal networking contacts, and some prosperity incense. After releasing the spell, my reinforcements included:

- calling at least ten stores a day to set up appointments to explain the products and offer them on consignment;

- writing each day to two or three networking contacts in different parts of the country asking for other potential outlet addresses;

- looking over the current product list to see which ones people bought most often, and why;

- writing up specific guidelines for custom-made, exclusive goods, including pricing;

- and creating a logo, slogans, and ad copy for advertising rates in catalogs that related to the products, including those on the Internet.

By following through on these reinforcements for an entire week, I gave the Universe at least seventy opportunities to answer my wish! And in the process I put a whole new professional polish on my business, which also encouraged continued success.

Magical energy looks for the most natural, simple route to follow in its manifestation. By making these types of regular efforts to follow up your wishes, you help carve out a path for your magical energy to return to you. Trusting in magic is one thing; putting your entire faith in a single ritual is quite another. Wishing is only one part of making dreams come true. Ongoing efforts must be extended to all levels of your being—physical, mental, spiritual—to achieve your wishes. Ideas and inspiration stagnate in your mind if they are not reinforced. Positive efforts and thinking provide that necessary reinforcement. Affirmative thought, affirmative action, patience, belief, resolve, and follow-through—these are the keys to success.

Imitative magic

There is a vast amount of historical evidence that firmly establishes the place of mimicry in the practice of magic. In ritual dance, painting, and sculpture, ancient and primitive cultures acted out or represented their hopes for prosperity, fertility, and much more. The idea, of course, was that if you imitated a successful hunt, or the coming of the rains or the act of procreation, you helped to realize it. The earliest imitative magic strove for oneness with the Divine which is just as important for today's culture as it was for those of antiquity. In *The Sacred Dance*, Oesterly explains that, "by associating yourself with [the Great Spirit], you are already in an indefinable way in communion with it. You have made friends with it." Something about the action of imitation makes the individual worthy of that communion.

The structure of society today creates certain self-doubts that consequently feed feelings of insignificance. Overpopulation overwhelms us in a swelling sea of humanity. Crime leaves us feeling powerless, without control over our fate. As a result, many of us have stopped believing in our ability to change the world. We need to reclaim that conviction, the feeling of worthiness, and imitative magic can help us.

The first step to recognizing our own Divine nature, and the life force abiding in all living things is to accept the fact that one person can really make a difference. Think of one cause you feel passionate enough about to give time and energy toward. Contact some people or organizations in your area that can get you started.

Before going about your tasks for this cause, take a moment out to pray or meditate and allow yourself to become a vessel for universal good. Let your work become a service to earth, humanity and the Divine. Believe in yourself and your efforts, and trust the Universe to meet you halfway in reaching your goals. Continue on this project for at least six months, noting your progress and feelings as you go. I nearly guarantee the experience will leave you more confident, hopeful, and fulfilled. Use this improved outlook to encourage results in your future wishing.

In *The Golden Bough*, Frazier writes that "things act on each other at a distance through sympathy." Likewise, acting out the fulfillment of a wish can bring you into physical and emotional harmony with it. Imitation identifies, confirms, and supports your wish today, and helps to define its future manifestation.

But, for whatever reasons, few imitative rituals from ancient times have survived. We have to create our own. Pantomime is a good option. Returning to the example of a wish for employment, you could mime the actions associated with your desired job as part of the spell. Or you could make gestures that are indicative of your intentions. If you wish, for example, for improved finances, you could go out and buy something associated with prosperity. Gourmet coffee or chocolates are two good choices. The actual expenditure can be minimal, but by buying something "luxurious," you behave as if you're already prosperous. Changing one's behavior requires mental participation, which also changes thought patterns. Magical outcomes will mirror the transition in your thought forms by becoming as positive and assured as you have become.

APPLICATION 19

Below you will find a list of wishes that seem to be very common to many people. I have provided illustrations of ways in which some of these could be acted out, and left the rest blank. Either on this page or in your journal, write down creative ways to reflect these goals through imitation. Usually the first thought that comes to mind is the one that will work best for you.

Goal	Imitative Component
Love	Giving yourself a hug or sending red roses to yourself.
Gaiety	Renting some humorous movies, exercising your cheek muscles!
Health	Eating nutritious food, participating in healthy activities like walking and aerobics.
Pregnancy	Wearing a pillow on your tummy, eating what you "crave" for a few days, and making love in a meadow.
Peace	_____
Happy Home	_____
Good Job	_____
Self-assurance	_____
Amicable Ending	_____
Earth Healing	_____

Imitative wishing does have its limitations. Be careful and think ahead about the ramifications of your wish. Social convention does not sanction passionately kissing a person you are attracted to at first sight, for example. On the other hand, you can make your feelings known with direct conversation to help open that door. If the individual responds, then your magic may turn a chance encounter into a relationship.

Imitative magic does not always have to be literal. In the previous chapter, I briefly discussed the use of spell components to amplify a wish's purpose. This promotes sympathy, to use Frazier's words. Let's return to our earlier wish for prosperity. The symbol of this goal is the collection of currency. To create the sympathy desired, you could tie some currency into a bundle with a long string and place it across the table from you. Then, as you visualize the fulfillment of your needs, pull on the string so the money "comes to you."

APPLICATION 20

Take the same list that is provided in Application Nineteen, and come up with symbolic alternatives to the actions you envisioned. For love, perhaps, draw two dolls embracing on a piece of paper. For gaiety put up smiling faces all around your living space and fill it with uplifting aromas. For health put a red cross on your door or keep canned chicken soup handy. For pregnancy consider the image of a stork. These are just ideas. Come up with symbols that have specific meaning for you.

Community wishing

It seems that magic doesn't have the same potency today as it did in the ancient world. One plausible explanation for this discrepancy came to me through a local spiritualist minister: population growth. The number of people on this planet are quickly overtaking its natural resources. This suggests that there is less natural energy per individual. The amount of magical power is being diluted.

If this is true, what does it mean in terms of community involvement? More individuals have chosen to work alone in recent years, for numerous reasons. I'm one of them. To achieve the loftier ambitions of wishcraft, however, we may need to gather our magical reserves, and share them through combined efforts. Whether directed toward personal or global intentions, a unified cry for aid can have startling effects.

A dramatic illustration of this concept appears in Katherine Kurtz's novel *Lammas Night*. It is a fictionalized account of the convening of a great coven of witches to keep Hitler from crossing the English Channel during the Battle of Britain. Historically, we know that Hitler changed his plans so as not to invade Britain at a time when he had the upper hand. To this day, people in the magical community of Europe credit the Cone of Power raised by the coven for this. Whether or not you believe the account, the meaning of the story is still valid.

We have been fortunate in our lives to see, firsthand, other examples of the wonders that can be achieved when people put their differences aside for a greater good. The Russian-American space mission is a notable example. I believe the magical community has a responsibility to extend similar efforts worldwide, only on a spiritual level.

APPLICATION 21

One of the most satisfying and universally appealing applications for community wishing is that of earth-healing. While litter pick-ups and recycling serve the body of Gaia—the Earth—her spirit likewise needs revitalization. For this purpose, a group of like-minded individuals may gather together and share their wish for a whole, united planet, then extend that wish outward to bless the earth and others.

The form this wish takes will vary from group to group, but one ritual that I enjoy centers around an old, healthy tree. The group gathers around the tree hand in hand. First, they breathe in unison to create a harmony of thought and purpose. Next, each person speaks one wish they have for the planet, like animal welfare or clean water.

Once the wishing goes full circle, visualization led by a chosen person may begin. This might take the form of a vibrant green light filling the tree from the top downward, then pouring into the roots, and from the roots out to the whole earth. Dancing clockwise, singing, and chanting may also be added to this ritual.

Afterward, each person should individually pledge to do one thing that helps the planet. For examples, my son does a neighborhood litter patrol that cleans up the sidewalk and yards once a week, my husband washes glass goods for recycling, and I'm trying to create a new project that will focus renewed awareness on the world's oceans.

If projects aren't feasible, consider a modest donation to an ecological organization. In the end, the enthusiasm of each group member can become contagious, bearing out the great power of wishing to change more than just our lives.

Wishing in classical literature

Fairy tales and other literary sources are filled with examples of wishing, many of which can be used to help you understand your own wishcraft. Writers often "drink from the psychic pool" for ideas and inspiration. Many do excellent research to formulate the magical procedures in their books. Two notable examples are Piers Anthony in his *Incarnations of Immortality* series and Katherine Kurtz in *The Derini Series* (DelRay Books), and *The Adept Series* (Ace Books, New York).

The Tales of the Arabian Knights is an example of classic literature in which magic is a central theme. In it, the Jinns bear a striking resemblance to the spirit guides and divine aspects we call upon in wishing. They are powerful, but have their limits. They cannot bring the dead back to life or force love, and they grant only three wishes, one of which cannot be a wish for three more. The Jinns are playful, too, like spirit guides and devas can be, requiring that you be precise and careful in your wishing, or else be prepared for the unexpected!

If you come across other examples of wishing or magic in your readings, make a note of them for future testing and application. Since many modern practices rely heavily on creativity, you can adapt any material, fictional or not. Some of the best resources in this regard are fantasy novels, role playing game guides (such as *Advanced Dungeons and Dragons 2nd Edition*, *Tome of Magic* and *Legends of Lore* by TSR), science fiction, and mythology collections. *Bulfinch's Age of Fable* is excellent for information on worldwide mythology and is a classic.

Meditate for a moment on the story of *Cinderella*. Here, a magical fairy godmother grants Cinderella's wish for a night of adventure. Why do you believe there was a limit on this magical charm? What steps did Cinderella have to take to break free from her bondage and find her wish's fulfillment? What lessons does this offer you personally in devising your wishcraft?

Think of *Sleeping Beauty*. In this story, what are the limits and consequences of malevolent wishing? How great is the power of both friendship and love in helping achieve one's wishes?

Consider the fable of *Pinocchio*. His wish for "realness" must be balanced with what other personal attribute for success? How and why do you feel Geppetto's wish manifested itself through his art? What does this say to you personally about the potential in your own art forms?

These are but three good examples from the stories of our youth that illustrate wishing, its powers, its limitations, and its by-laws.

Evoking spirit guides and symbols

Wish magic can evoke the elemental assistance of Jinns and other powerful guides. In Arabic folklore, each type of Jinni has a specific elemental domain. The Effrete, for example, is a fire Jinni, prone to explosive emotions, that wears bright reds and golds. When set free, it explodes in a mass of flame and sparks. In European and American tales, there are the capricious, whimsical fairy folk, who can be generous, but also love to fool unsuspecting humans. For example, sprinkling buckthorn by the light of a full moon is said to bring an elf who grants one wish. Returning for another, however, results in a century-long nap! (See Froud and Cunningham in the bibliography.)

Preparation and discretion should be used any time you call on elemental or devic creatures for aid. They are entities of raw drive whose motives are foreign to us. Under no circumstances should you call upon them without first setting up a proper sacred space.

And don't request their assistance without a very good reason. Additionally, the elemental spirit you call upon should somehow have a connection with your wish. Fire elementals can help with energy, passion, and wishes for dramatic change. Earth elementals are good for helping things grow or finding good foundations. Water elementals work well with the emotions and instincts, and air elementals are best for wishes pertaining to humor, movement, and the conscious mind.

APPLICATION 23

In preparing your sacred space for elemental contact, make certain first that a symbol of the element you seek is present. Like attracts like. Having a representation of earth, air, fire or water gives you something physical to focus on and provides the creature with a specific point of manifestation. Here are some examples:

Earth	a potted plant; a globe; a bowl of rich soil; a rock; incenses like musk with rich, earthy aromas; items which are dark green, brown, or black and rough.
Air	an open window; wind chimes; feathers; a paper or electrical fan; incense with very light aromas; items that are pale yellow, white, or blue and gauzy.
Fire	a brazier; incense burner; fireplace; red candles; oven; raw wood fire; incense with spicy aromas; items that are orange, yellow, or gold.
Water	a hose; water faucet; fountain; glass of water; rice sprinkled like rain; sounds of rain on tape; water plants like lilies; items that are deep blue or green.

Next, you will need to prepare yourself mentally. Within your sacred space, begin deep, vibrant breathing and quiet meditation. Direct your resolve so that nothing but the current task is in your mind. Take as long as you need to rid yourself of mundane thoughts, pressures, and tensions.

Now focus on the element you have chosen. If earth, for example, feel the cool soil upon your skin. Sense the power of flowers, trees, and other living things that the soil feeds. Envision the element as a brownish-green sphere of light before you. Let this sphere grow until you almost sense a personality about it. This sensation is the first sign of contact.

You will know an elemental's presence by sight, a distinct change in the air, sounds, and sometimes texture. A fire salamander might signal its presence by heating up the room or visually appearing as a bright incandescence. A water undine sometimes turns the air damp or causes a liquid's surface to ripple. These physical manifestations make the entity more comfortable and signal successful contact.

After you invoke an elemental presence, concisely give it your request. This can be achieved by reaching out toward your visualized sphere or physical manifestation and channeling your desire in that direction. Be polite, precise, and respectful. If the elemental needs to communicate with you, it will usually do so on a telepathic, emotional, or gestural level. You may hear melodic sounds like tinkling bells for an air elemental, forming a rough facsimile of your language. Emotional messages are intense, the typical form for volatile fire and impassioned water elementals. Gestures may take the form of a game of charades.

Once you have finished your request, do not tarry any longer than necessary. If the elemental agrees to help you, simply thank and release it. I mention this because it is tempting to ask a lot of questions of such entities. It is also tempting to stare at them for a while because they can be exceptionally beautiful. Even so, the faster you get around to explaining your task, the more quickly they can respond, and get back to their other responsibilities.

If you truly want to spend extended time with the summoned entity, ask if it can stay. Your honesty will be appreciated. Don't be surprised if the answer is no, however. You have already diverted it from its other tasks and given it more work, so additional delays may not be acceptable.

Make notes of your successful encounters in your journals for future reference.

If you are uncomfortable with calling on these creatures for aid, consider employing elemental symbolism as a focus for your spells instead. Here, instead of evoking a specific entity, you direct your energy to an appropriate elemental symbol to convey the wish.

Each element has a personality that suits different types of spells. Water guides your wish smoothly along the course you've carved out for it and focuses on the spiritual nature. Fire provides intense energy, especially for transformation, and focuses on the subconscious, untamed nature. Earth provides a solid foundation for abundant progress, and its focus is on practical matters. Air gives flight to your dreams and encourages activity, but not always directly, and focuses on the conscious mind. Also, the direction of the wind can create additional elementary symbolism. The north corresponds to earth and leisure, the east to air and beginnings, south to fire and maturation, and west to water and circulation.

APPLICATION 24

Here are some examples of spell topics and possible elemental correspondences. Below them are several more without an elemental association. Meditate on what these themes mean to you and which element would be best for your goal. For the purpose of this exercise, you might want to take note of the reasons why you chose a specific element.

Wish	Element
Wealth	Earth, so money can grow
New Job	Air for movement, earth for solidity, or water for smooth transitions
Healing	Fire to purify or water for gentle cleansing
Peace	Water to calm angry fires or air for fresh perspectives
Hope	_____
Fertility	_____
Forgiveness	_____

Friendship	_____
Finding a lost item	_____
Success in a new project	_____

Since rice is a potent symbol of providence and abundance in Asian cultures, you might use it, for example, as an alternative to calling upon an earth elemental by grabbing a handful while you make a wish. Afterwards, plant the rice in rich soil with the seed of a flowering plant. Tend it with love, reiterating your wish with each watering, invoking the water element. Give the wish more energy by leaving the plant in a brightly lit area to invoke the fire element.

Techno-wishing

While superficially it seems that technology and magic are antithetical concepts, the two can work together quite harmoniously. Consider for a moment that many of the hopes and dreams of people 100 years ago have become today's realities. If these people could see the technical advances we take for granted, they would call them magic. The power of wishcraft helped bring many of these wonders into existence, as inventors and creators acted on their visions with true conviction! By combining spiritual approaches with elbow grease and technology, we can conceivably begin to build an even better future. My favorite illustration of this is computer "magic."

Right now hundreds of like-minded people are linked through the Internet. Isn't this medium a potentially great vehicle for wishcraft as a community project? Couldn't friends conceivably hold long-distance rituals, or send spell energies to one another by figuratively downloading the magic with e-mail? Magic's electrical energy blends with this technology in amazing ways.

Couldn't your computer's password reflect a wish? Choose a word or phrase that symbolizes your goal, then each time you sign on the system, you reiterate your wish! Document files have similar potential. For example, name your files "peace," "victory," "prosperity," or "health," then retrieve those energies every time you open the files.

Some people might not like the idea of putting their journal or diary on a disk, but it can make your life easier, and it saves paper. You can update, revamp, and reorganize your information in much less time than handwriting takes. If you decide to try this yourself, don't overlook interesting fonts. Some have magical-sounding names and visual characteristics that can enhance a spiritual procedure.

You can use **BOLDFACE** to represent courage, and subscript or ~~strikeout~~ for banishment. People who have good printers can also consider symbolic watermarks or color to further empower the visual impact of their hard copies. If you have a good symbolic imagination, the possibilities are endless.

Don't automatically turn off your spiritual side the minute you hit the on button of your computer. Find innovative ways to make technology a friend and partner in wishing.

A P P L I C A T I O N   2 5

Make a list of all the technological items you have. Next to each item come up with a word or short phrase that exemplifies its potential use in your wishing. For things that you actually want to use in the sacred space, write up a brief description of those uses. Here are some examples to help get you started:

Television/Computer Screen: We already anticipate seeing profound things on this surface through conditioning. Try meditating on a blank screen and using it as a crystal ball.

Use the screen as an affirmation bulletin board by placing self-adhering notes with positive phrases or spell emblems on it too.

Microwave Oven: Place components that won't be harmed by the microwaves in the oven to saturate them with the "fire" element. When you need fast outcomes, a microwave becomes an excellent symbol since we already associate it with quick turn-arounds.

VCR/Tape Recorder: Tape your rituals for group members who cannot attend. They can then enjoy indirect participation afterwards when they receive the recording!

If you have a hectic schedule that does not allow much time to repeat spells, record them and play the tape while you're getting ready for work, making dinner, or whatever. Again, this is indirect participation, but the energy you put into the initial work will be released each time the tape gets played. Since you are listening to the words, this reactivates your mind to focus on that goal.

Electrical Lines: Since these run throughout an apartment or house, they can carry your magic along with the electrical current to envelop and protect your home. Extend a wish for safety or peace as an electrical function of the brain, then channel that energy towards an outlet. Continue guiding the energy by visualizing the electrical network releasing light into every room of the house. Add to the effect by turning on lights in every room as you go.

Technology need not be a destructive force if it maintains a connection with the Sacred. We are accustomed to separating our spiritual lives from everyday reality. But looking at science and technology in a new way, we can reclaim the unity of body-mind-spirit-life that makes for effective wishing and positive, responsible living.

Vocalized wishing

As mentioned in the previous chapter, there are numerous forms of vocalization that may be applied to wishing. Some of these techniques have very long histories, and are found with minor variations in many cultures. The three most common forms for spiritual vocalization are chant, mantra, and song.

Chant:

The ancient Greeks, Mesopotamians, and Egyptians all used chanting in religious observance as a way to connect with the originating force of the Universe. The word "chant" comes from the Latin *canere*, meaning "to sing." Typically in chanting several words are applied to one tone.

One commonly known chant is the *Tibetan Om*, a sacred syllable representing and affirming the eternal soul that exists throughout the Universe. In Hindu tradition it is spelled *aum* and represents the three-fold divine name. For wishing you may use the Om chant to center and focus your awareness or create your own brief, simple phrase. The resonance of your words will carry the energy out from yourself towards the spiritual horizon. The chanting should be repeated with as small a break in meter and sound as possible until it naturally crests and dies down.

APPLICATION 26

To determine what tone can best sustain a chant, listen to the sound you make when you yawn. This is well within your vocal chords' relaxed, natural range. Chants work most effectively when you're not straining to maintain a pitch.

Take a deep breath filling your diaphragm from the bottom up. Slowly release this air with your chant so that each word comes out evenly. Keep the chant phrase short enough that you can say it at least once with each breath. Continue the cycle of deep breathing and release, feeling the energy rise.

Don't try to force the chant. If it takes on a more musical quality, if new words come out spontaneously, if you feel the need to move with the words, just let these things happen. It's part of the sacred energies you're building. Eventually the pace will slow again of its own accord and you will know you are done.

A synonym for chant is "psalm" which comes from the Greek word that means "to pluck." This is a fascinating linguistic signifier. When someone chants they actually begin tuning the body's cells and the molecules of the sacred space to a specific wish's frequency. The act of releasing the sound then becomes analogous to plucking the tuned harp of self to engender the desired results.

Mantra:

Originally mantras were chants consisting of Vedic hymns or text, designed to improve inner focus. One myth from India talks of the god Rama blessing his shaft with Vedic mantras to fight and conquer Ravana, a high ranking demon. Similarly, in Persia, the

Zoroastrians recited *Ahuna Vairya*, which they believed would guarantee a light-filled victory. Today, in New Age spirituality, the definition of a mantra has expanded slightly to include any words or sacred syllables spoken in rhythm to improve meditative states.

APPLICATION 27

Find a location where you can be ensured of some privacy for a while, and where you can openly chant without feeling self-conscious. Sit in a comfortable position, but one in which your back is straight. Loosen your clothing a little bit for ease of breathing. Breath is vital to effective mantras and chants.

Next, take a few, deep, even breaths to relax and center yourself. Then, try reciting the word Om with each exhale. As you do, pay special attention to how this syllable makes you feel in various parts of your body, and also on an emotional level. See if these impressions change after 10, 20, or 30 repetitions of the word. Make note of these feelings in your diary.

Next, intone each vowel of the alphabet similarly. Repeat each one 10, 20, and 30 times noting the way the vowel resonates in your head and heart. Some people find that this brings on tears, laughter, or sudden flashes of insight. That's because the vibration of the sounds release memories from our body. Once these blockages are released, sacred energies flow more smoothly and return us to a balanced state.

In wishing, mantras may be chosen to correspond with the vibrational needs you have. If, for example, the vowel "o" makes you feel more open and intuitive, and your wish is for more insight, then intone the "o." The word Om and vowel "i" generally promote self awareness and growth. The way you personally react to each of these sounds, however, will be as individual as you, which is why the first part of this application is so important. Your experience can then guide you on choosing the right sacred sounds for your wishes.

In my own experiences, I've found that mantras can come to us quite unexpectedly. During meditation one afternoon, I found my mind filled with what sounded like words, similar to the Christian experience of "speaking in tongues." After looking up these "words" in various foreign language dictionaries, I found they told me much about the nature of my soul and its travels. Now, whenever I find my sense of self getting lost, I recite this phrase three times and it brings me back into center.

I mention this because mantras can have many other spiritual applications besides your wishcraft. Be open to the words, phrases, or sounds the Universe provides during meditation. They may prove helpful in all your metaphysical pursuits.

Song:

Similar in form to chanting, songs are made up of many more tones and complicated patterns. And although they may be more difficult to master, they have at least one advantage. There is probably already a tune somewhere whose words reflect the goal of your wish. If need be, you can repeat only the portion of a song that most specifically talks about your wish, turning it into a daily affirmation.

I know that some people feel awkward about their singing voices. If so, perform your vocalized wishing alone, or in the company of trees. I did this as a child, and the trees never complained. Also, don't worry about being off-key, the Universe hears only your intentions.

APPLICATION 28

If you find you cannot find a song that adequately conveys your wish, try an alternative tact. Pick out a children's tune with which you're familiar. Ones like "Twinkle, Twinkle Little Star" or "Mary Had a Little Lamb" work quite well. Using the chosen song's sub-structure, you can now create what is known as a "filk." A takeoff on the word "folk," filking means putting new words to old songs.

The most effective filks for magical purposes are those which maintain the meter of the music. To be certain you do this, count the syllables in the given words of the song, and then substitute new words that have an equal number of syllables. Lining up the natural stresses of the new words with the music helps with the flow. Obviously, the words chosen need to reflect as many details of your wish as possible, within the limits presented by the music itself.

After you finish constructing your ditty, sing it as often as possible, whenever you are doing anything that may help bring the wish to fruition. Write it in your journal, it may be helpful to you or someone else again in the future.

Here's a magical filk I created for a bartender whose car broke down:

Original Verse	Filk Rendition
Mary had a little lamb	Tony needs a working car
little lamb, little lamb	working car, that goes far
Mary had a little lamb	Tony needs a working car
whose fleece was white as snow	so he can tend the bar

The wish was not extravagant, but vital to Tony. He needed a car to keep his job. He sang the filk while riding on the bus, while looking at vehicles, and while reviewing automobile advertisements in the paper. He found that it kept his attitude upbeat and hopeful, so he didn't get discouraged when the first two days proved fruitless. On the third day he found a reasonably priced car. The owner had to move away and was even willing to set up private financing!

Artistic wishing

Art mediums provide tremendous outlets for giving your wish a visual, finished form. Art begins with your imagination; it is non-linear, just like magic. Its scope is limited only by the artist's talent and the viewer's perceptions.

In exploring artistic media, you also explore the depths of personal vision, your soul, and the creative spark that lies within both. Once that spark is released, it gives energy to all your inventive expression, including your wishing. As your work on your art, it slowly takes form, eventually becoming as tangible as you want your wishes to become. It is an affirmation that you can see and touch repeatedly until the wish manifests. The completed project may also inspire and help others achieve their dreams.

Carving:

The process of carving is unique among the creative visual arts. In painting or assemblage art you add material until your piece is complete, whereas in carving you take material away. Many people who carve tell me that they are only chipping away what doesn't belong, that they are able to see the finished work of art in the medium.

Soft woods and soapstone are two excellent materials for beginners, both being fairly easy to work with. The tools you use are chisels, rasps, and files.

APPLICATION 29

Obtain a piece of wood or soapstone large enough to carve out a *sigil* or symbolic representation of your wish. Place the medium on a table in front of you. Turn it and look at it from all sides. As you do, unfocus your eyes and try to see your completed representation in it.

Take a moment to bless your tools, breathe deeply and maintain a meditative state while you carve a representation of your wish. If it helps, pray and chant as you work. Go slowly. Continue with the piece over several days if necessary, until you sense your work is done. You will intuitively know when this is. Leave the object where you can see it often to remind you of your wish, thereby energizing the magic further.

Please note that this application can be adapted to any of the artistic mediums you wish to try, and it can be repeated at any time you feel the need to support, redirect, or emphasize your magical energy.

Some people find they are disappointed by the results of this technique, anticipating an object that looks like David, and getting one that looks more like Gumby! It's important to remember that the intention of your work, and the magical energy it generates is far more important than the art's aesthetic appeal. Magically speaking, an emblem is no less powerful than what it represents in the sacred space. With this in mind, your time and efforts are never wasted.

Collages:

Cut out pictures that portray various aspects of your wish in the ideal, completed form and arrange them symbolically on poster board. Take your time, and let your instincts guide your hand. When you find an arrangement that resonates, finish the collage and leave it somewhere that you can see it regularly. This will provide a positive visual image to focus your energy with.

Model Making:

Using clay, balsa wood, or building blocks in all their commercial variations, model-making allows you to represent your wishes from the foundation up, watching the progress each step of the way. These are more "concrete" art mediums, well-suited to wishes invoking new homes or renovations, or motor vehicles.

Needlecraft:

The power in needlecraft comes from two sources—the patterns it creates and the knots. Patterns are symbolic representations of energy. As they are knitted or sewn together, the final picture literally weaves the strands of your wishes into a finished form. Any knots or finishing seams bind the energy of your wish into that object, which then becomes a perfect talisman to carry with you. They also make nice gifts into which we place our good wishes for the recipient.

Painting:

When painting your wishes, sometimes it helps to close your eyes first and get a full, three-dimensional portrait in your mind. Exactly how this comes out on canvas depends on your ability with a brush, but be it symbolic or realistic, your imagery can help you direct your mental energy toward supporting your wishcraft. And as with other wish art, if your finished painting is displayed, every time you look at it reinforces your wish.

Music:

Music is a naturally vibrational, universal language that can create a harmony of purpose within and around your working area. Drumming is particularly suited to domestic creative wishcraft because it requires nothing more than your hands, a sense of rhythm, and a metal pot from the kitchen!

APPLICATION 30

Gather everything together that you want to use in your wish spell. Create the sacred space, and put the components together. Then sit with anything that can be used as a drum (even the surface of a table will do) and begin to meditate on your wish. As you do, let the wish resonate out of your being with each beating of your heart and every breath you take. Hear this sacred rhythm, which is also the pulse of the Universe, and begin playing it on the "drum" surface.

Allow the visualization to become more three-dimensional and your focus to deepen. At this point, a chant or sacred song may be added if you wish. As this process continues you will notice the rhythm naturally increasing until it reaches a pinnacle. At this point lift your hands from the surface and move them out from yourself, pouring positive energy out through your fingertips towards your goal. It sometimes helps to envision this energy as a sparkling wave of colored light, or one which is shaped like an arrow so it finds its mark.

Note how you feel after this experience. It will probably leave you slightly drained, so don't stand up too quickly. This is a good sign. It means you effectively channeled your wish outward to begin its work.

I have only recently discovered drumming as a spiritual tool, but it is truly a wonderful one. If you ever have the opportunity, talk to drummers at a ritual gathering and have them share their insights on the Tribal Soul. You will not soon forget their words. You might also consider buying a drum, if this form of expression suits you. It makes a versatile, personal component for a variety of rituals and is well worth the investment.

These are only a few of the numerous art mediums you can apply to your wishcraft. If you aren't familiar with what's available, take a brief trip to a local art supply store. If you find you really enjoy one particular medium, think about taking classes in it. Your craft could become as personally fulfilling as it is spiritually.

The meaning of "crazy" ideas

Some wishes may indeed be inappropriate. Need is an important prerequisite for successful wishcraft, therefore any wish that is not the expression of a clear need has to be considered carefully. Does that mean that something we only desire, but don't truly need shouldn't be an object of wishing? I believe that magic guided by love and respect for all beings will rarely overstep its bounds. Greed and a hunger for power have no place in wishcraft, but I don't think there is anything wrong with employing magic to make our lives happier and more fulfilling, even if the idea behind it seems a little crazy.

Some wishes appear impossible because of our circumstances. On the other hand, all wishes are based on our dreams, no matter how grand. Individuals who regard their wishes as too outlandish to materialize will rarely act on them. By doing so, they fail to take advantage of an opportunity for their magic to express itself, and they discount their own potential to make a "crazy notion" work.

It does not appear viable to wish for employment as an oceanographer, for example, if you only have secretarial skills. Your wish becomes plausible, however, if you return to school to study oceanography. You have taken the "wild idea" and given it a solid foundation from which to grow.

APPLICATION 31

Think back to the many times in your life you've thought to yourself "I wish," but discounted the idea almost immediately as being "crazy." If possible, try to remember three of these. Return to Chapter One and follow the fourteen-step plan for effective wish spell creation. Put together everything you need for the magical part of the equation for each wish you've recollected. Think about the practical matters. What needs to happen physically, socially, mentally, emotionally, etc., for this wish to be viable?

Please realize that you may have to change your entire lifestyle to achieve a "crazy" goal. However, anything really worth having is also worth working for. After some serious consideration, you can decide whether or not to go forward with the wish magic.

By combining the rational mind with intuitive, magical energy, wishing allows us to reach beyond the "believable" with assurance. Through the same process, it also may provide a means to explore the uncharted abilities of the mind. Medical research on placebos has shown the importance of faith in healing oneself. But what about the bigger picture? What happens when we not only believe in our magic, but act upon that trust?

We can live our dreams. We can dare to hope. In the end, wishing allows you to rediscover a part of yourself that believes in miracles. More importantly, it shows you that miracles don't just happen to other people; they can happen to you, and be manifested by you!

PART TWO

Wishing Guide

How to Use the Wishing Guide

Thy silent wishes to results shall grow,
and day by day shall miracles be wrought.

—*Ella Wheeler Wilcox*

Wishcraft is a highly personalized practice in which the individual practitioner determines the significance of its symbols. This section contains two alphabetical listings, one of wish symbols and traditions, and one of deities, from several cultural and religious sources. Each entry in these lists is followed by an explanation of its origins, its historic uses in wish magic, and suggestions for its use in your wishing. But these lists are not meant to be the final word on wish symbology as it applies to your work. It is up to you to determine which, if any, of the symbols and deities are appropriate to your wishing. It is also up to you to determine if the traditional associations of those wish components are relevant to you.

For example, suppose you have a garnet that you always carry for good luck. The entry for garnet says it is a component for wishes related to health and happiness. Accordingly, you have the potential to add the garnet to any wishing ritual, charm, spell, or visualization for luck, well-being, or joy. Of these goals, however, one for good fortune will probably bring the most success, because that's what the stone symbolizes to you. In any case, beginning your magic with a personal token, one already filled with your energy, inevitably improves results.

In addition, don't overlook the folk traditions you may have heard about from relatives and friends. These wishing customs frequently can't be found in any history book—they are a unique oral tradition. As such, these are potent tools, not only for wishcraft but also for continuing your family's legacy. Here are a few other guidelines to help make your wishcraft more consistently successful:

1. Avoid attempting any wishes when you are sick, angry, or out of sorts. These feelings are powerful and can overshadow your efforts.

2. Once you're mentally and spiritually primed for wishing, find one word that describes the essence of your wish's goal. Examples include "love," "happiness," and "finding." Keep this word in mind while researching possible components for your wishing spell, ritual, or meditation.

3. Review the lists of components and deities, noting those traditionally most suited to your goals. Assemble as many of these as you deem practical and appropriate in one spot to be blessed and charged before you begin.

4. If you can't find any symbols or representations on the lists that you really feel comfortable with, create your own!

5. Determine the best way to utilize your components and representations. For example:

   • Use them as part of a visualization

   • Use them to create incense

   • Use them as symbols of your desire to be burned for divination, released to the winds or water for movement, or buried to grow (Just take care that any items used in this manner are environmentally safe)

   • Use them to make emblematic foods or beverages to internalize the manifesting energy

   • Use them as offerings to a specific deity

   • Use them to decorate the altar and sacred space to visually remind you of your goals

- Use them to make portable charms, amulets, and talismans

- Use them as focals

- Use them as dramatic props

- Use them to make creative gifts

6.   Keep a notebook detailing your efforts, and their progress. I suggest a 3-ring binder for cost-effectiveness and simplicity. This way, as you update, change, and adapt your wishing traditions, you can easily pull out and replace sheets.

7.   Any time you have questions or concerns about procedures review Part One for assistance. Or look at books that detail ritual and spell procedures such as *To Stir a Silver Cauldron* by Silver RavenWolf, *The Spiral Dance* by Starhawk, *Spinning Spells, Weaving Wonders* by Patricia Telesco, and *Earth Magic* by Scott Cunningham.

8.   Repeat your wish spell any time you feel the need.

9.   Get excited! Emotion is a powerful motivator.

10. Relax and have fun. Wishing brings out the inner child in each of us; the child who believes in the unseen world and dream land. This youthful energy is very potent and very refreshing. Let it transform your life.

11. If possible, find partners to participate in the wishcraft to increase its power.

12. When your wish does come true, don't forget to thank the universe for its gifts. Light a candle, say a prayer, share your bounty with another, and count your blessings. This is a step all too often overlooked in a world of instant gratification. Every day can be a miracle in the making if we approach it with grateful spirits and hopeful hearts.

My wish for you is the greatest success!

*Myths are clues to the spiritual potentialities
of the human life.*

—*Joseph Campbell*, The Power of Myth

Listing of Wish Symbols
and Traditions

Acorns

Acorns are good luck charms. This belief probably comes from the Druids, for whom the oak tree was sacred.

Acorn tops can be drilled with small holes for stringing into decorations or jewelry. As you work with them, keep a strong image of your wish in mind. Then place the strings where they can visually reinforce your wish, or wear them to bring luck.

If you have the space, try planting an acorn with a symbol of your wish in rich soil. Care for it religiously. As it sprouts, your wish should start to manifest. Plant the sprout in the forest and bless the earth as a way of thanksgiving.

Agate

The Lithica attributes agate with the power to fulfill wishes for men and bring love to women. Cardani, a sixteenth century writer, recommends carrying agate to increase one's riches. Among early rural communities, moss agates were worn on the right arm while plowing to ensure a plentiful harvest.

Consequently, agate is very suited to wishing aimed toward improving relationships, finances, and fruitfulness. Use this stone in personal power pouches, spell boxes, and jewelry, or place them around your house (see also *Spell boxes*).

Almond

· · · · · · ·

In Sweden, tradition has it that if you receive a whole almond in your rice pudding, you are to eat it and make a wish for love and marriage.

The almond tree is featured in the Greek myth of Demophon and Phyllis. Demophon returns from the Trojan Wars and meets a beautiful princess with whom he falls in love. Their romance is interrupted when Demophon has to travel back to Athens for his father's funeral. He promises to return by a certain day, but misjudges the travel time and is three months late in arriving. In the mean time, Phyllis, thinking herself abandoned, hangs herself. The gods are so moved by her love that they transform her into an almond tree. Demophon offers a sacrifice to this tree, declaring his love, and the tree responds by blossoming.

To this day almonds remain symbolic of undying love. This is why many marriage receptions have almonds as party favors.

Amaranth

· · · · · · · ·

A flower of dark purplish-red, the Greeks believed some of these blossoms never die. If one makes a crown of Amaranth, then recites their wish, the flower will bring Divine favor. Amaranth comes from the Greek word *Amarantos*, which means unfading.

Dried amaranth petals are good for casting to the winds with wishes or adding to a wishing incense to speed manifestation and divine intervention.

Amethyst

(see also *Onyx*)

In the Middle Ages people used this stone to cool passion or tame unruly natures. Carry or wear it during your wishcraft to regulate energy. Crown the tip of a magical wand with an amethyst for strict regulation of your wish's energy.

According to legend, this stone gained its deep purple hue from a draught of Bacchus' cup that rendered it so beautiful, it charms anyone who views it.

Amulet

To make an amulet that brings a wish into reality, use the two halves of a walnut shell. Inside, place a bit of sage, ginseng, seven shelled sunflower seeds, and the tuft of a dandelion. Secure the two halves with sturdy glue, then carry the token with you. Each amulet may only be used to aid one wish. Create a new one for your next endeavor, placing the old in the soil or on a sea shore (see also *Walnut, Sage, Ginseng, Sunflower seeds,* and *Dandelion*).

Angelica

(see also *Tea*)

According to folklore, the plant angelica was a gift given by the angels themselves. The medieval herbalists recommended this herb to heal many of the most dreaded diseases of the day.

To internalize the energy of your wishes, drink a cup of angelica tea sweetened with honey. The honey adds blessings and a hopeful attitude (see also *Honey*).

Ankh

In ancient Egypt, the ankh was held in the right hand when making a wish for rain or fertility (see Budge in the bibliography). In hieroglyphics, it means "that which cannot die." It was a principal amulet for bodies of the dead, thought to ensure a safe journey for the deceased's spirit. It was also depicted regularly with images of gods, goddesses, kings, and queens.

Apples and apple seeds

(see also *Seeds*)

The apple tree was sacred to many ancient gods and goddesses, who bestowed miraculous attributes upon its fruit. Our saying, "An apple a day keeps the doctor away" is a vestige of that high regard.

On Halloween, which is the Celtic New Year, if while bobbing for apples, you're the first to bite one, make a wish, then eat it for good fortune.

To find out if your wish will come true, heat up a few apple seeds. If they pop and fly, it is a hopeful sign (see also *Fire*).

If there are thirteen seeds in an apple that you are eating, it's a sign to make a wish.

According to English folk traditions, a farmer should always leave at least one apple in a tree for the fairy folk during harvest. If they take kindly to the offering, they will aid in a wish's manifestation.

Carefully slice an apple crosswise to reveal a pentagram pattern. Make several of these slices and dry them. Add them to wishing pouches and incense, hang them in windows as a decoration, or plant them in the earth to encourage your magic (see also *Incense*).

Apron

(see also *Clothing*)

Victorian women would turn their aprons inside out at the time of the new moon to change their luck and make a wish. During this era, the apron was considered a sign of domestic bliss and contentment. Since aprons are seldom worn these days, try it with any piece of clothing.

Ashes

(see also *Fire*)

In Armenia, ashes from the sacred fires honoring Mihr, a solar deity, are spread around homes, barns, gardens, and fields on the night of February 26th with a wish for prosperity. This tradition mirrors many other spring observances worldwide, wherein fires welcome the sun, and the ashes from the fires bless the land or farm animals. Beltane on the first of May is one notable example (see also *Beltane, May Day*).

To best gather the energy of these fires, sweep from the outside of the ash circle into the middle then collect the pile. These ashes also have a practical use—they provide your garden soil with nutrients.

Ash leaf

(see also *Leaf, Clover*)

If you find an ash leaf with an even number of divisions, pluck it while making a wish, then wear it in your hat, a button hole or carry it in a pocket until the wish comes true. It is as powerful as a four-leaf clover.

The Norse believed that the ash tree was actually the fabled Yggdrasil, whose roots feed the earth.

Aspen

(see also *Leaf*)

According to Saxon tradition, place an aspen leaf under your tongue if you wish to improve your capacity for communication. In ancient times, this was also thought to heal muteness (see Black in the bibliography). Plant some near your home to protect it from robbery. In Germany, aspen was laid on graves to prevent the spirits of the departed from wandering.

Astrology

(see also *Moon*)

While astrological timing may not ensure a wish's fulfillment, it can certainly help. Among the ancient magi, it was common to watch the signs in the sky to know the best timing for any magical endeavor. These signs were not limited to the placement of the planets, but also incorporated unusual lunar phenomena and grand occurrences like comets.

One excellent example is the practice of making a wish when one first sites a "blue moon." This is the second instance of a full moon in one month, a very rare occurrence. The rarity of the event was believed to increase its power to influence human affairs.

To know what astrological timing is best for your wish, consider its theme. Then look for that theme in an annual astrological calendar or moon sign book. These sources contain a wealth of useful information to consider in your wishcraft.

Some astrologers claim it is best to make wishes when your ruling planet is governing, or on a date that numerologically equates to your lucky number, using either a single digit or a combination. For example the 13th = 1 + 3 = 4, the lucky number for Aries. Lucky numbers for each of the astrological signs are:

Aries:	4	Leo:	5	Sagittarius:	8
Taurus:	9	Virgo:	3	Capricorn:	2
Gemini:	7	Libra:	6	Aquarius:	3
Cancer:	2	Scorpio:	8	Pisces:	4

Ax

According to the *Old Testament*, you can use an ax when you wish to find treasure. Get a round agate. Heat the head of an ax in a fire until it's red hot, then place it so it's sharpened edge is upright. Try to balance the agate on it. If the agate stays put, there is no treasure in the area. If it falls off on the same side of the ax three times, the treasure lies in that direction. If it falls off on different sides, you will have to search the entire region (see also *Agate*).

Badger

In voodoo and Gypsy traditions, placing a badger's foot beneath someone's bed ensures adoration. An cruelty-free variation would be to use a picture or carving of a badger instead (see Spence in the bibliography).

Among Native Americans badgers are respected for their ability to dig in the soil, symbolizing a talent for finding hidden things and an intimate knowledge of Earth. They also have very powerful jaws, indicating self-expression and the importance of sacred stories. Therefore, use this imagery when working wishcraft for communication and discovering the truth.

Balasius

This reddish-purple, semi-precious stone from Northern Iran is mentioned in the *Enchiridion* of Pope Leo X, a collection of charms and prayers from the 16th century. For people wishing to increase their love or reconcile a quarrel, this crystal should be exchanged as a token.

Bamboo

In China, people made bamboo flutes to charm spirits or to use for divination in their temples. It is said that if you inscribe your wish on bamboo and bury it, the wish will manifest. Bamboo may have gained this powerful reputation in the East because the wood never changes color, indicating strength and resilience.

There is a folktale that claims bamboo was originally formed by the Lord of the Tide to aid the Prince of Heaven on a quest for his brother's lost fishing hook. In this story, the bamboo made a water-tight basket the Prince could float in on his journey.

Bamboo can be symbolically used in any wish where long-lasting results are desired.

Banana

Banana is a wishing fruit. Make your wish, then take a bite. Or cut a slice from the stalk end, and if a Y-shaped mark appears in the banana at that point, the wish will come true.

Among the people of India and in the islands of the South Pacific, the banana is a sacred food, offered to the gods and valued as a bringer of luck. It is especially effective in wishes for literal or figurative fertility and fecundity.

Basil

Basil is sacred to the Hindu god Vishnu, and finding it is considered an omen of happiness. Chew a fresh leaf while making a wish for joy.

Hang bundles of it in your kitchen for the practical benefit of shooing away flies.

Bay laurel

(see also *Leaf*)

Bay leaves were used by Apollo for prophesy. Write or draw a representation of a wish on a bay leaf and burn it, thereby releasing your wish to the Greek god.

Bay laurel was sacred to Greco-Roman deities. Crowns made of it were placed on the heads of victors in the Olympic Games. Wear one when enacting wish spells to help bring success.

A Gypsy tradition suggests writing your wish on the back of a bay leaf and keeping it enclosed safely in a box. When the wish comes true, your are to burn the bay leaf in thanksgiving (see also *Spell boxes*). If you get a whole bay leaf in your soup or stew, make a wish and take a small bite of it. The bay ensures your success and provides extra energy for its manifestation.

Bean Throwing Day

In Japan, the faithful bring lanterns to the Kasuga Shrine in Nara, where they are lit on Bean Throwing Day, February 4th. People dedicate each lantern to a loved one and inscribe it with wishes for that individual. The glow of the lantern is symbolic of hope and a belief that the gods will see and answer the prayer.

A Western alternative might be to light a candle carved with words representing our wishes on this date. Remember, however, to make wishes for others, too, in keeping with the Japanese tradition (see also *Lantern, Candle*).

Beans

(see also *Tonka beans*) ,

The ancients believed those wishing for prophetic or visionary dreams should not eat beans or other "inflating" foods. Both Plato and Pythagoras espoused this, feeling that the animal nature had to be quiet for such a wish to be fulfilled. You might want to avoid beans for several days before attempting wishcraft, especially those spells pertaining to foreknowledge and intuition.

Among African tribes mojo beans are sometimes carried for wish fulfillment. For this, two beans are carried for three days, then thrown into moving water on the fourth day. Within one week the wish is believed to manifest.

Bee

(see also *Honey*)

In Louisiana, a yellow honey bee flying around a person is said to portend the fulfillment of a wish or other good news. In many ancient cultures, bees were considered divine messengers, thus their unexpected appearance at any affair was not taken lightly.

The next time you see a bee sitting on a flower, whisper your wish in its general direction so it can take the missive directly to the Divine.

Beech

Inscribe your wish on a piece of beech wood and bury it, leaving it undisturbed for one year. If the wish does not manifest by that time, it was not meant to be. People may have regarded the beech tree as particularly powerful because when two of its branches lay against each other they often meld and grow together.

Bells

(see also *Flute, Drum*)

Ring a bell eight times during, or at the end of, your wish spell. Eight is the number of completion and manifestation. Bells traditionally amplify power, symbolize the creative force, and announce your intentions to the Universe. In Buddhist tradition, paradise has melodies played by the daughters of the gods who are accompanied by a thousand ringing bells. If a bell is not available, consider using a drum similarly, which is a shamanistic receptacle for Spirit.

Other musical instruments may function for this too. You can, for example, pluck a string on a harp or guitar eight times. Sufis say "Music leads the soul to the highest realm. It enables us to bridge the gap between man and god" (see Chapman in the bibliography).

Beltane

(see also *May Day, Sun*)

Save all your wax remnants from magical candles throughout the year. On Beltane, tie them up in colorful tissue paper with a bright purple ribbon. Hold the bundle in both hands while making a focused wish, then release the cache into the Balefire. As it burns, the positive magic from the rest of the year provides energy for manifestation (See also *Ashes, Candles, Wax*).

Beltane, falling on May 1, is used for this activity because of its associations with spring, rebirth, and fertility. This is traditionally a fire festival where the returning sun is honored.

Beryl

Beryl is an excellent stone to use as a talisman or part of a medicine pouch for those wishing to improve their likability and motivation levels. It is also good for the safety and protection of travelers.

Beryl was written about extensively in the 13th century by Marbodus, and again in *De Proprietatibus Rerum* by Thomas de Cantimpre during the 19th century. Both writers described beryl as a stone that was so potent as to render its bearer unconquerable.

Bes
· · · ·

In ancient Egypt, people carried images of this dwarfish god of good fortune to help manifest their wishes and bring divine favor. Bes was small in stature, round, and ugly-faced, and he could scare away any malicious energy that might impede a goal.

Bible
· · · ·

Think about a wish you recently made, then randomly open a Bible. Look at the first word on the left-hand page. If the word has an even number of letters, your wish will not come true. If it has an odd number of letters, however, divine favor is on your side! This technique is a form of bibliomancy, or divination by books, that may use any book for an answer. Presumably the Bible provided more definite answers because it is a sacred text. You can substitute another book more appropriate to your own beliefs for this exercise.

Birds
· · · ·

(see also *Blackbird, Crow, Feather, Goose, Ladybug, Turkey, Robin*)

In merry Old England, a woman looking for a husband would capture a "lady bird" (ladybug), then bid it to fly in the direction of her future beloved.

If you hear a bird singing to the west of you after making a wish, it is said to be a good sign that your wish will come true. With this in mind, feathers could be a potential token for wishes focused on finding a soul mate.

In Southwestern Native American lore, if a bird overhead drops a feather as it passes, this grants you one wish from any bird of that type. Two restrictions exist. First, one must keep the feather and present it with the wish, and secondly, the wish must be suitable to the type of bird it came from. For example, a seagull could protect one from drowning, or perhaps help with a fishing expedition.

The importance of birds for European magic probably dates back to the times when they were viewed as harbingers. The word "auspice" (and its adjective "auspicious") comes from a Latin word meaning "bird observer." Both the ancient Greeks and Tibetans had extensive texts on how to interpret bird omens.

Bird seed

(see also *Seeds*)

Hold these in your hand while concentrating on your wish, then sprinkle them clockwise for growth, blessing, and increasing wishes, or counterclockwise for decreasing and banishing wishes. Birds will grab the seed and take your wish to the gods.

Birth stones

(see also *stones* by their specific names)

In the first century A.D., Jewish historian Josephus wrote about zodiacal stones being connected with those of the ancient Hebrew priests' breastplates. His ideas were echoed by St. Jerome in the 5th century A.D., but the custom of wearing birth stones did not become popular until sometime in the 18th century.

Once this became a tradition, it was believed that wearing your birth stone, or carrying the stone associated with the current month, could help fulfill your wishes by attracting good luck. The only stone this wasn't the case for is the opal, believed to bring ill fortune to all but those whose birth month it represents.

Biting your tongue

If you suddenly realize you have misphrased your wish, or made one in error, bite your tongue lightly. This is a countercharm that keeps the energy from escaping your lips, and also keeps evil spirits from hearing the mistake. Another approach is snapping your fingers to break the spell.

Blackbird

(see also *Birds*)

If you see two blackbirds sitting together, make a wish. In some European locales this is considered a very good omen. Seeing swallows and wrens is also considered quite lucky, the wren having been sacred to the Druids.

Blood

Blood is potentially one of the most powerful components in any magical ritual. An individual's blood acts like a precious sacrifice to the gods, asking for aid. In modern wishcraft, other items of a deep red color or with similar symbolism may substitute. Using blood root or beet juice is an example. While arguably this is not as personal, magically speaking, a symbol is no less potent than what it represents.

Generally, for best results the blood or blood substitute should be dabbed on an item that represents your wish. This marks the item with your life-energy, which naturally carries your wish within it.

Bloodstone

(see also *Jasper, Carnelian, Agate*)

In the 19th century text of *Specilegium Solesmense*, bloodstone is recommended as an amulet for wishes pertaining to improved respect and leadership abilities, and for people who want to discern falsehoods. According to *Curious Lore of Precious Stones*, a 1907 treatise by Kropatschek called *De amuletorum apud antiquos usu* states that this stone grants the bearer whatever they request. Similarly, the *Leyden Papyrys* indicates that bloodstone carried as a talisman is a wish-fulfiller. It is important to note, however, that when these writers referred to a "bloodstone" they may have been discussing red coral, red jasper, carnelian, or red agate.

Blue

(see also *Color*)

An old children's saying states "Touch blue and your wish will come true." This may have something to do with the fact that blue was considered a protective hue, being the welcome color of fair skies. Blue, the color of the Wode plant, was also an honored color among Druids who used it to dye their belts, color tattoos and mark Celtic warriors.

Boat festival

During early April, the children of France launch small boats on the Rhine River with masts made from candles. This boat transports good wishes to whomever finds the ship and brings it ashore. In your own home, you can use floating candles in the bathtub instead! (See also *Candles.*)

A similar event takes place in China on June 8th, when full-sized boats are adorned with charms, especially those to frighten away evil spirits. Then boat races commence in honor of Ch'u Yuan, a 3rd century scholar who protested the evils of the reigning court. Afterwards, the contestants eat a feast of rice dumplings for good fortune.

A readily available alternative would be eating rice cakes found in the cereal or bread aisle of your supermarket as part of a wish ritual or spell on this date. Rice is particularly suited to wishes for prosperity and providence.

Bottles

While "messages in a bottle" have often been depicted as cries for aid from someone on a deserted island, in wishing, it is likely to be less literal than that. Toss your bottled wish directly into the whispering sea to ask its gods for a response.

Jinns were sometimes found in ornate bottles in classic literature. The beauty of the bottles was partially due to their magical properties, and the more precious the bottle, the most precious the prize (see also *Gold, Silver*). Additionally, the shape of a bottle closely resembles the womb, the source of life, from which magic may be born.

In the interest of ecology, I suggest hallowing out a piece of wood instead of a bottle, placing your wish inside on biodegradable paper, and then corking the ends. This will carry your wish on the waves, but not harm the ocean.

Bowl, brass

In an ancient Shinto ritual of Japan, pieces of paper are placed in a brass bowl containing a magical fire made by a priest called a *maeza*. The priest inscribes the papers with descriptions of the sickness an individual wishes to banish. While the embers burn, they clap their hands to get God's attention. Afterward they place the ashes on another piece of paper to symbolically indicate their success.

Adapting this slightly, when wishing to rid yourself of a bad habit or illness, write that problem on paper. For added effect, you may write a word describing the problem backwards, upside down, or and in letters that diminish in size or number. For example, *smoking* can be written like:

gnikoms

gnikom

gniko

gnik

gni

gn

g

Burn the paper, then sprinkle its ashes counterclockwise (for banishment) around yourself so the magic of your wish can fly on the winds.

Bread
· · · · · ·

(see also *Rice, Pasta*)

A special unleavened bread wafer called *oplatek* is served in Catholic Polish homes during *Wigilia*, a Christmas feast of the Vigil. This wafer is stamped with images of the nativity. As it is passed around the table, each family member breaks a piece off. A friend of mine reports that in her home this was accompanied with a silent wish for the coming year.

If you cannot find a recipe for *oplatek*, consider using a loaf of homemade bread or pita. Mark the bread before baking with a symbol of your wish and let it rise with the heat. Eating the loaf then internalizes that hope.

Gypsies carry small bits of bread in their pockets as they travel to ward off danger. This may have developed from the use of "journey cakes." These biscuit-like tokens lasted for a long time, which was a necessity when travel wasn't swift. Dry bread or a biscuit, therefore, could be an excellent component in travel-related wishing. Put a piece in a special pouch to take with you. Or drop crumbs along the road leading to your house while focusing on your wish for a safe journey. The birds will enjoy your treat, and the blessed crumbs magically mark a safe pathway to return by.

According to *Superstitions and the Superstitious*, Europeans give their children bread bits at an early age, while making a wish for their continued health. You might want to add bread bits to any Blessing-Way ritual, or other special magical ceremonies where good wishes are extended to the children in your life.

In certain Egyptian locales, it is considered very fortunate to find a piece of bread, the symbol of life. When found, the bread is supposed to be touched to the lips while whispering a wish, then touched to the forehead (the third eye). Finally, for the wish to come true, the finder must magnanimously give the bread to a stray dog, thereby sharing divine blessings (see *Dog*).

On New Year's Eve, place a loaf of bread and a penny on your dining room table while wishing for providence (see *Coins*). This ensures that you will not want in the coming year (see Hand in the bibliography). Try choosing the coin's year to focus the magic according to personal needs. For example, if you need more providence in your home, choose the year in which you moved to that residence. Or if your daughter is away from home and having trouble finding a job, use a coin depicting her birth year.

Carry salted bread into a new home for luck and providence. Pretzels are a good substitute! This tradition comes from Germany. It is probably due to salt's preservative nature and the belief that salt is a safeguard against evil.

Place freshly baked bread on your window sill and make a wish while you spread honey on top. If this appeases the fairy folk the bread will be gone by morning and your wish will manifest by the next full moon.

Jews eat a smooth loaf of bread on Rosh Hashanah, the Jewish new year, as a wish that the coming year will be smooth and prosperous for the family (see also *New Year's*).

Bread is a traditional food of kinship and sharing (see also *Rice, Pasta*), so its near-universal use in magic is understandable. Romans fed flat bread to their armies to aid physical strength. This may have had something to do with Pliny the Elder's belief that fermented bread made with yeast would deplete the body. In the Middle Ages, bread was associated with wealth, since only those of means could afford white breads.

Any one of these many correspondences can be used according to the goal of your wishcraft. If you need improved strength, for example, make a wish for vitality while nibbling on fresh flat bread. Or to encourage new friendships, toss bread crumbs on the ground and let the birds give your magic movement.

Bridal bouquet

(see also *Flowers*)

The flowers of a bridal bouquet should be secured with knotted ribbons, which represent the wishes of the bride's friends for her happiness. When this bouquet is tossed, the person catching it should make one wish for the bride and undo a knot in one of the ribbons for that wish to come true (see also *Knots*).

Bridge

(see *Crossroads, Rainbow*)

If a train or airplane passes over a bridge while you're driving beneath, put your right hand to the car roof and make a wish. This superstition comes from the ancient belief that arches and other similar structures were magical meeting places. Bridges also symbolize the divide between the physical and ethereal worlds, so they give your wish added power to reach the Divine.

Another bit of lore suggests that if you make a wish at one end of a bridge, close your eyes, and navigate to the other side while holding your breath, your wish will come to pass. It will indicate, at least, that though you may be foolhardy, you are lucky!

Broom

Romanian tradition has it that a broom placed beneath a pillow or bed sweeps away negative influences, encourages serendipity, and keeps nightmares firmly at bay. The herb broom was originally used to clean the home, and was an ancient symbol of domesticity, mature womanhood, and fertility.

To make a wishing broom for your home, find a full-sized or miniature broom in a good craft or hardware store. Decorate the broom with items that represent your wishes. Examples include roses for love, sprigs of lavender for peace, or numerous green, leafy items for prosperity. Leave the broom readily visible, charging it with positive energy each time you see it until your wish manifests. Afterwards take the emblems off and either give them to another in need, or ritually dispose of them. You may decorate the broom again for your next bit of wishcraft.

Buckthorn

European traditions say that if you sprinkle buckthorn in a circle by the full moon, an elf will appear and grant you one wish. That is, if you happen to see him and ask quickly enough. It might be helpful to bring along a bit of sweet cream or cake to entice him.

Dioscorides, a Greek physician, wrote about the virtues of buckthorn and recommended it for keeping away all enchantments and wizards. This is an odd reversal from the folk wish shown above, in that instead of keeping away a magical creature, the buckthorn is used to call and command it!

Butterfly

If a butterfly lands on you, tell it your wish, especially one that is to spiritual in nature. In ancient times, butterflies represented the ascending soul and the Triune nature. They carry your wish's energy on their wings.

Raising a wishing butterfly can be a fun activity for children. The fat, green caterpillar you find on milkweed, for example, will "magically" become a Monarch butterfly through metamorphosis. Keep the caterpillar in a well-ventilated area with plenty of food for it. Each day the child should talk to the caterpillar, and share his or her wish with it. Eventually the caterpillar will spin a cocoon, which symbolically "spins" the magic. When it finally emerges as a Monarch butterfly, have the child release it, voicing the wish one last time to liberate energy for manifestation.

Cactomite

(see also *Carnelian*)

In Greece, this reddish stone (probably a variety of carnelian) was carried to ensure victory in battle. Its name comes from a Greek word *kaktos* meaning thistle, a protective plant also of reddish-purple hue. If your wish pertains to success, achievement, and victory, consider incorporating a piece of carnelian as a component.

Cake

In Greece, a wish to find a lost item was accompanied with a fruit cake. These sweets, made of spices, honey, brandy, and grated orange rind are offered, along with a wish, to St. Fanoureo, the patron saint of "lost and found." Should the item return to its owner, the cake is then taken to the church to be blessed and shared with the poor. This is easily adapted to wishcraft by simply substituting a patron god/dess for the saint, and then sharing the cake with some-one in need. Additionally, the ingredients of your cake may be cho-sen to symbolize the lost item or object of another wish.

During the Middle Ages, people broke the wedding cake over the head of the bride to wish for many children and marital "sweetness." The custom had its origins in Rome where more crumbs meant more children. The roses on the wedding cake were an additional wish for abiding love. Each of these traditions can be added to a modern handfasting or wedding with little difficulty.

The tradition of birthday cakes dates back to ancient Greece and the worship of Artemis, a moon Goddess. Each year the day of her birth was celebrated by worshippers with moon-shaped, honey cakes adorned with candles (see also *Honey, Moon*).

Candles, birthday

When blown out, birthday candles release the celebrant's wish with their smoke to the winds. This may have some connection to the ancient use of incense and other perfumes to represent spirits or to convey one's prayers to the gods. It may also be linked to early rites for Artemis, to honor her sacred fires (see Tuleja in the bibliography).

A friend recalls that in her home, different birthdays brought dif-ferent wishes. Her grandmother instructed that on the 13th birth-day one should wish for love, money, and health. On the 16th birth-day, for a mate. In the latter instance, the candles were put under the celebrant's pillow for three days so the perfect mate would appear in dreams within a fortnight. On the 21st birthday, wishes for good jobs and independence were made. Additionally, as the candles were lit, one wish per year, i.e. per candle, was made. The last one lit was the first candle snuffed out. Afterward the candles were bound into a charm with ribbons, a lock of hair, a dollar bill, a rose, and a favorite trinket from childhood. These were carried to the river and tossed in for luck, symbolically to make the break from childhood.

Use birthday candles annually to reaffirm life and make a positive wish for the coming year. Pattern them symbolically for visual effect. For example, place them on the cake in the form of an eye for wisdom. A carrot pattern on a carrot cake works for improved insight.

Candles, yellow

(see also *Color*)

If you wish to hear from someone in a hurry, push a new needle deeply into a yellow candle. Secure it close to the wick using a thimble. Inscribe the individual's name on the taper, concentrating intently on that person with each letter carved. Light the candle and let it burn all the way down. Usually the person will call before the candle goes out, or within 48 hours of casting the wish.

Car

If you see a green car, cross your fingers and make a wish. This tradition may have originated during the time when cars were still rare.

Carbuncle

(see also *Garnet*)

Getting its name from the Latin word for coal, carbuncle is a smooth, convex garnet believed by many ancient cultures to be a peacemaker. Should two friends have a disagreement and wish to make amends, this is the perfect stone to exchange in a ritual. It additionally ensures the bearer of good health.

In the *Koran*, the fourth heaven is made from carbuncle, and among Christians the deep red stone was used to illustrate the concept of Divine sacrifice.

Carnelian

Alfonso X in the late 1880s wrote that carnelian grants luck and hope to women, and that it is a powerful talisman for those who want to speak courageously. This belief may have come from the fact that Mohammed, according to tradition, frequently wore a carnelian ring that he used as a seal.

Add carnelian to spells or power pouches for wishes concerning communication, leadership, or good fortune.

Carrots

Eat glazed carrots on New Year's Day while making a wish for joy. These will bring sweetness in the following year. This belief may have its origins in Scotland, where carrots have their own holiday, Carrot Sunday. Farmers bring carrots to the church on that day to be blessed. Forked ones are considered to be the most fortuitous. Families then take the vegetables to their home the next day for eating. This celebration used to take place in September as part of the harvest festivals that preceded the Celtic New Year in October, now known as Halloween. That makes September a good month in which to add carrots to your wishing (see also *New Year's Day*).

Carrots were also prized among the ancient Greeks who regarded them as a potent, effective aphrodisiac, so they may play a role in love wishes too.

Cat

In old rural England, some people believed that one may make a wish when they meet a black cat in passing and stroke it. This act of kindness is said to help your wish come true. More than likely, this bit of wish lore was connected with the idea that cats were witch's companions with mysterious powers.

The idea that cats brought luck could have originated with the ancient cultures of Egypt, China, and Arabia. The Egyptians had a cat-faced goddess named Bast. Confucius was known for his love of cats, and Mohammed preached while holding a cat.

Caudle

(see also *Glogg, Wassail*)

During the Middle Ages, this beverage of gruel and warm ale provided sustenance to travelers when food was sparse. Because of this, it was customary to make a wish for providence when toasting the caudle cup, in hopes that a real meal might be found in the next town. This tradition was noted in the *Form of Cury* (circa 1400), a manuscript prepared by members of Richard II's court.

For contemporary practices use oatmeal or ale as spell components in any wish for prosperity, improved luck, hospitality, and safe travel. For best results, part of it should be consumed, and the rest poured out as a libation.

Ceromancy

(see also *Wax*)

To discover the answer to a nagging question, or to know if a wish will come true, try divining by wax or ceromancy. Melt good quality wax in a brass container over a low flame (double burner style works best). Pour the liquid slowly into another vessel filled with cold water while concentrating on your question.

As you pour the wax, solid dot-like patterns will form on top of the water. Interpret these images as you might an inkblot. For example, perhaps you recently made a wish for love. Should the figure of a heart appear on the surface of the water, this is a good sign. If the heart separates into two, then the relationship may only be temporary. Similarly, if your question has to do with how long you will wait before romance blossoms, and two dots form, this can indicate a span of time such as two days, two weeks, two months, or two years. Smaller dots indicate smaller increments of time.

The ancient Greeks, among others, practiced this form of divination (see Loewe in the bibliography).

Chalcedony

(see also *Quartz*)

This is a type of lightly colored quartz with a waxy finish. If your wish pertains to success in legal matters, carry this stone with you. In the Middle Ages, chalcedony was kept by those who wished to keep away phantoms and apparitions. Additionally, the black variety is said to give the bearer clear, concise speech.

Chalk

Mayans of Yucatan draw a chalk line from the tomb of a deceased loved one to their hearth. This ensures the spirit can return home whenever they wish.

Applying this to wishing, draw a chalk line on a piece of recycled paper from yourself to a picture or word that symbolizes your goal. Recite your wish out loud as you draw. Keep this paper in a highly visible area, repeating your wish each time you see it. When your wish comes true, then burn or bury the paper.

Champagne cork

In Scotland, the cork from a bottle of champagne drunk on a special occasion is saved. It is then split, and a silver coin is placed in the crack, while making a wish for health, wealth, and happiness.

Charm

In Dahomey (West Africa), people fill a sack with red and white kola powder. This is soaked with pigeon blood at dawn as a wish is recited. The charm is then carried until the wish manifests. It must be resoaked to aid a new wish.

This tradition uses the power of blood as a central symbol. A more cruelty-free alternative would be placing a carving of a bird, a pigeon's feather, and a few drops of beet juice in a sack. Any white and red powder or grain may be a substitute, but it should fit with the theme of your wish.

Chimney sweep

While no longer a common sight, chance meetings with chimney sweeps were once thought to be very fortuitous. In England, one would spit after seeing the sweep, then make a wish. Presumably the spitting kept evil spirits from hindering the wish.

Chimney sweeps may have been considered lucky for several reasons. Unclean chimneys often cause fires, so the sweep may have been associated with fire safety. This may also have been a result of the early worship of fire, in which anyone showing power over fire would be respected (see also *Fire, Iron, Horseshoes*).

Chopsticks

During Chinese New Year, chopsticks are used with a special meal of rice, mandarin orange, fruit seeds, and flowers. Each of the items in this meal represents a different wish for the family. The character for chopstick means "to be present" and is a symbol for unity. Mandarin orange is for luck, and seeds and flowers represent continued fertility.

Try preparing similar symbolic dishes for yourself and your loved ones on special occasions. For example, on the date of a wedding anniversary, eat foods symbolic of love and passion like two chocolate-covered berries or two heart-shaped cookies.

Christmas

(see also *Yule*)

During the Victorian period, it was common to make wishes while stirring the Christmas pudding. For it to be effective, the stirring had to be clockwise. One wish was made for each month of the coming year. This was also done with the Christmas cake batter (see also *Cake*). Adopting this for today, it might be particularly fun if each family member added one ingredient and stirred while making a wish. Try this on birthdays too!

The time of year we celebrate Christmas was particularly important among many ancient civilizations of the northern hemisphere, because of the Winter Solstice. From this point forward days get longer and nights get shorter. Early forms of the solstice celebration heralded the return of a reborn sun, the symbolism of which was not lost on early Christian theologians.

Chrysanthemum

(see also *Flowers*)

Gather the small black centers of a chrysanthemum at dawn's first light. Steep them in an equal amount of warm (not hot) oil of roses. Store in an air tight container. Anoint yourself with this oil daily to empower and realize wishes of amiability and acceptance.

The term chrysanthemum comes from the Latin meaning "gold flower" (see also *Dawn, Summer Solstice*). In China and Japan, eating chrysanthemums and drinking wine made from its petals is believed to increase one's longevity. Rural Americans regarded chrysanthemums as a meeting place for the Fey.

Chrysolite

(see also *Topaz*)

Also known as olivine because of its green color, the early French used chrysolite or peridot to ward off nightmares and fear. For this purpose it is best set in gold. If you wish concerns banishing personal anxiety, wrap a small piece of peridot in gold cloth and carry it with you (see also *Gold*).

According to legend, the original source for chrysolite was the Serpent Isle in the Red Sea. The gem could only be found by night, when it radiated, marking the spot to dig for it the following day. The gem was well-loved by Egyptians, and eventually it was prized in Europe as "booty" from the crusades. Some historians believe that the chrysolite spoken of in many accounts of the crusades, however, was actually topaz.

Chrysoprase

The Greeks called chrysoprase the "golden leek." The Greek word *chryso* means gold, and *prason* means leek (see also *Leek*). This green and gold stone brings joy and health to the bearer. If you yearn for happiness or improved zeal, chrysoprase is an excellent component to consider for your wishcraft.

One story recounted by Albertus Magnus may be the source of chrysoprase's reputation. According to it, Alexander the Great wore this stone in his girdle when going into battle to ensure victory.

Clay

Ancient stories from many cultures tell of all life coming from clay. In Egypt, for example, animals and people, even the gods were said to be born of the Nile's rich clay.

Make an image of your fulfilled wish out of clay, then let it harden. If you can't make a literal representation, make some type of figurative one, like a rune or other magical sigil. Leave the image in the light of the sun or moon for seven days, depending on the goal of the wish. Solar energy is best for conscious, logical, lawful matters, while the moon is best for the intuitive and emotional. Once the wish comes true, either pass the image on or ritually destroy it.

Clockwise movement

Our ancestors felt that moving in a direction that follows the path of the sun through the day was helpful in any positive magical endeavor. Examples can be seen in superstitions about stirring clockwise when baking a cake or passing a wine bottle clockwise when serving. This can likewise be used in your wishing to improve overall results (see also *Days, Wells*).

Clothing

My grandmother said that if you accidentally put something on backward or misbutton an item of clothing, it was a very fortunate sign. Make a wish before you fix it. However, if you don't discover the error until after you leave the house, walk backward, retracing your steps and re-enter the house before changing things around. Otherwise it will bring bad luck.

One should make a wish whenever they don a new item of clothing. Additionally, if the clothes have a pocket, put a coin in it to encourage plenty (see *Coin, Firsts*).

Clover

If you happen across a four leaf clover, make a wish while picking it, then carry it until the wish manifests. Then it is best to share the clover with someone else in need of a little good luck.

Four leaf clovers were originally sacred to the Druids who felt that someone who had one could see demons and prevent any harm from them.

Coal
· · · ·

see also *Fire*)

Back in the days when coal was delivered to homes, finding a piece was considered auspicious. To make a wish on it, the finder held it, spat on it, then burned it in the hearth. Fire releases a wish.

It is interesting to note that in Old England pieces of coal were sometimes put in Christmas socks to allow the recipient to make such a wish. It has only been in recent years that receiving coal in one's stocking has come to indicate "naughtiness."

Cock
· · · · ·

(see also *Birds*, *Feather*)

In Arabian, Persian, and Slavonic cultures, the cock is a ally who warns of the presence of evil spirits. Therefore, it may figure into any wishes you have for safety and protection. If you come across a feather from a cock, carry it with you for safe travel.

In Scotland, a black cock was used by sorcerers to bring rain, and thus might be a good symbol for weather-related wishes.

Ancient Greeks pronounced the name of the cock to cure ailing pets and livestock. Romans used the tail feathers to open locked doors and as a sacrifice to the plural deity Lares. In Asgard, the Norse version of heaven, a cock awakens departed heroes daily. Accordingly, the picture of a cock may help in wishing for animal health or welfare, opportunity, and guardian energy (see Cooper in the bibliography).

Coffee

If there are bubbles in your coffee, try to capture them with a spoon. If you succeed, you may make a wish, especially one for improved finances. This tradition may have come to us from Arabia, where coffee is a hallowed beverage, and where bubbles in a vase or vessel indicate the presence of a jinni.

Coins

(see also *Gold, Silver, Copper, Tin*)

During the Victorian era, to find a penny with the year of your birth on it was thought to bring luck and entitle you to a wish. Coins were added to many charm bracelets as a symbol of fulfilled wishes.

Around the same time in Europe if one heard a cuckoo and had money in their pockets, the tradition was to turn the coin or purse while making a wish. Similarly, at the first sign of a new moon you should turn a silver coin while reciting your wish.

Keep a special jar by your door. Every day for a month, when entering and leaving the house, place a coin in it and repeat the same wish. At the end of the month give the money to a good cause to release its energy.

Coins were first used in magic and wishing because they were made from precious metals. Anything valuable to humankind was also considered of value for offerings to the gods (see *Wells*). And finding coins was certainly a sign of good fortune in a world where the majority of people were poor (see also *Gold, Silver, Copper, Tin*).

Color

(see also *Blue*)

Various colors are mentioned in wishing traditions. Most often they are chosen to emphasize the correct energies for the type of wish being made. Here is a brief list of associations:

Red:	energy, passion, power, vitality, protection
Orange:	friendship, outcomes, a less vigorous form of red
Yellow:	creativity, insight, communications
Green:	growth, money, fertility, abundance
Blue:	peace, healing, wisdom
Purple:	spiritual matters, leadership skills
Brown:	grounding, sowing new attributes
Black:	banishing, drastic transformation
White:	protection, purity, drawing positive energy

Color is one of the most superficial of all wishing components, but it can enhance the natural energy of any symbol used in magical procedures. Consider any of the following examples for their color possibilities, then choose those that are most sympathetic to your wish's goal:

candles	clothing	soap bars	linens
beans	jewelry	paper	paints
buttons	crystals	toys	feathers
fabrics	artwork	candies	shells
foods	light bulbs	flower petals	beads

Cookie jar

A friend of mine recounts this story: "As a child, I was allowed to write out a wish note on my birthday. This went on the most beautiful paper I could find, accompanied with a pinch of glitter and a picture of the situation for which I wished. The paper was then folded up as small as possible, and put under my pillow for one night. The next morning, I placed the wish in a cookie jar purchased for the family by my great grandparents.

Finally on New Year's Eve, we spread out grandmother's shawl and dumped the contents of the jar on top. Each person picked out their wishes to see how many had been answered. While I suspect mom peeked to help fulfill some of those hopes, many others were not easy to facilitate. Even so, some of those wishes were met too.

Today, I still keep a wish jar for my family. I often burn wishing incense in front of it, especially on the New Moon, Full Moon and other special days. At the end of the year, I'm always surprised by how many wishes have come true."

Copper

(see also *Coins*)

Draw the image of a letter G as shown in the Persian Magi alphabet inside a six pointed star on one side of a copper piece. On the other, draw a dove inside a six pointed star (see also *Birds*). Bless this with violet and rose incense and keep it in a green or rose silk container if you wish to bring love and harmony to your relationships.

Corn

To know if your wish will come true, grab a handful of dried corn kernels. If you have an even number, the results will be positive. If an odd number, the timing of your wish may be poor, and outcomes are questionable.

On Lammas in Scotland (August 1), people gathered around ritual fires to honor the harvest. They wore circlets fashioned from corn husks that were tossed with a wish on the flames at the end of the celebration. Corn was likely used in this activity because of its strong associations with prosperity and divine providence in rural communities.

To make such an activity even more meaningful during any celebration or observance, fashion your circlet out of items that represent your wish. As each burns, they carry the message of need to the Universe.

Couscous

(see also *Corn, Rice, Pasta*)

A hard wheat semolina, couscous is eaten in a ritual fashion in Algeria and Morocco. People hold their spoons in the right hand and eat from outside the bowl inward. This leaves the center of the dish always full as a silent wish for heavenly blessings. Couscous is, in effect, regarded similarly as corn and rice in other cultures.

You might want to try this with any wheat cereal at home, finally giving the last bite to a pet or the birds outside so they can transport your wish. As you bless others and the earth, so shall you be blessed! (See also *Birds*.)

Cow

(see also *Milk*)

In India, *Nandini* is a legendary wish-fulfilling cow who gives milk and a healthful elixir to those who seek her. Among Indians, an offer of milk from someone should always be accepted as it is the beverage of *Lakshmi*, the Goddess of fortune.

Consider milk as a spell component when wishing for prosperity, serendipity, or well-being. Use the image of a cow as an empowering component (specifically through visualization) for health-related magic.

Cowslip

(see also *Flowers*)

Those wishing to unearth treasures either literally or figuratively should use this flower as an amulet. German folktales say that the cowslip originally formed from St. Peter's keys. Thus they open many doors, revealing anything hidden.

Cream

People in rural Europe often left out offerings of cream and honey breads for the "wee folk" while making a wish. Frequently this wish had to do with minor chores getting completed. If the cream and bread disappeared, it was a sign that the fairies accepted the gift and would attend to the wishes (see also *Bread*).

Crocheting

Infuse a skein of yarn with your wish. Crochet (or knit) the yarn, visualizing your wish in manifested form as you work. This should come to fruition in 21 days.

To reverse the process, like wishing that a streak of bad luck would end, unravel a row of the crochet fabric each day while visualizing the changes necessary. An alternative for those who do not knit or crochet is cutting off the top of an old sock and unraveling it.

Crossing your fingers

(see also *Fingers*)

The easiest way to make a cross, which was an ancient talisman symbolizing the four directions and four elemental powers, is to cross your fingers. At the juncture of the two lines, a wish may be held safe until it comes true. This seems to be the case for lies too, as people cross their fingers behind their back when telling untruths to keep them safe from discovery.

Crossroads

Bury a coin or other token of your wish at a crossroads and it will come true within a fortnight. Make sure to travel to and from the site in strict silence (see also *Coins, Silence*).

Since ancient times, crossroads were regarded as potent locations. They were sacred to the Greek goddess Hecate. The Celts considered them an excellent place for divination and prophesy. Pagans regarded them as symbolic of the four elemental powers. And Carl Jung explained that crossroads symbolize the Mother Goddess.

It is also said that you may meet the devil at a crossroads at midnight to exchange your soul for a special wish.

Crow

(see also *Birds*)

If you see a crow in flight, make a wish. If the bird continues on its course without flapping, your wish will come true. If it flaps, however, look away quickly or the wish may not come to pass. This type of omen interpretation was prevalent in Tibet where the crow is considered a Divine messenger.

Dactylomancy

This is a type of divination that uses a metal ring attached to a long piece of thread or twine. Place an image of something that symbolizes your fulfilled wish on a table. Hold the string with the metal ring in your strong hand above the image. Steady the ring with your other hand, then let go and concentrate on your wish. Movements forward and backward are positive signs that the wish will come true. Movements left to right (side to side) are negative omens.

Daisy

(see also *Flowers*)

Most people have heard of plucking daisy petals and saying "He/she loves me, he/she loves me not." This can also work to determine the outcome of a wish. Think about your wish, then pluck the first petal with a "yes," the next with a "no," and so forth, alternating until the final petal is plucked and you have your answer.

The daisy may have been used for such divinatory practices because of its old folk name "day's eye." It gained this name because of the way it follows the sun's movements. As seen throughout this text, the sun has been a central spiritual force in most civilizations and cultures (see *Clockwise*).

Dandelion

(see also *Flowers*)

Blow on a dandelion gone completely to seed to release your wishes to winds. In the Victorian language of flowers, dandelions are the bearers of prophesy, and if all the seeds fly free on your first breath, your wish will come true. If a few seeds are left behind, the wish will take some time. Many seeds left behind indicate a wish that is not granted, or one that may have unforeseen ill effects if fulfilled.

Dawn

The beginning of a new day, when the first rays of hope beam across the horizon, is considered a particularly potent time for making wishes. This also seems to be true of dusk and midnight and noon, which are traditional "in-between" hours when the veil between this world and heavenly realms grows thin. Of these, dawn and noon are the most positive, when the sun is on the ascent and when it has reached its highest point in the sky.

Some wishing traditions also instruct the participant to face east, the direction of the rising sun, when making their wish. These beliefs regarding daylight and the sun may also have some connections with the symbology of fire or fire sources (see also *Candles, Fire, Pyromancy*).

Days

(see also *Dawn*)

In Ireland it is believed there is one hour in each day when a person can see spirits and get wishes fulfilled. This hour is only discovered by trial and error (see Farrar, 1990 in the bibliography).

Of all the days in the week Sunday and Thursday seem most auspicious for wishing. Sunday gained its reputation by being ruled by the sun. Thursday is governed by Jupiter, the largest, luckiest planet and the Supreme God of Roman mythology. It is particularly good for business and financial wishes. Other days of the week may be used in timing your wish as follows

Monday:	matters of intuition, travel, change, and anything that requires quick results
Tuesday:	matters of law, bravery and initiative
Wednesday:	matters of kinship, and self promotion
Friday:	matters of romance, love and home
Saturday:	matters that are strongly effected by timing

Dew

If you wash in the first morning dew on May Day make a wish. Generally, this tradition is best for wishes pertaining to love, beauty, and fertility (see also *May Day*).

Gather this dew by draping out a linen cloth carefully over two chairs so the middle is exposed to open air. Wring the dew out into ice cube trays and freeze it to keep the magic "fresh" until it's needed.

Diamond

The diamond gained its mystical reputation due to its hardness and rarity. It was highly valued among many early cultures, including those of Arabia, Persia, Egypt, and Greece. For example, in an Orphic poem, the diamond is recommended as a charm for wish fulfillment. For the charm to work, the gem must be worn, and is best when received as a gift.

As an interesting aside, the gift of a diamond to a Buddhist temple is thought to ensure that the giver reaches nirvana—where the soul is absorbed into the Supreme Spirit—upon their death. It may, therefore, be useful as a wishing gem for matters of spiritual growth, charity, and inner wisdom.

A less expensive substitute for a genuine diamond is the gem known as a herkimer diamond, which is a very clear type of quartz.

Dice
· · · ·

(see also *Seeds*)

In medieval Europe, people tossed dice to determine the outcome of a wish. If they rolled three sixes in a row, their wishes for an entire year would come to pass. Two sixes in a row indicated some adversity. Tibetans have a similar technique using three dice, but for them the number eleven portends success.

Using dice for divinatory purposes is a very ancient practice, documentable back to 1500 B.C.E. Egyptian legend credits the outcome of a dice game between the Moon and Thoth with extending the year from 360 to 365 days. In Greek myth, gods rolled dice to determine who won specific portions of the Universe.

In other civilizations, different forms of dice were used. Assyrians had ones made of clay, and the Babylonians used bone. Sumerians used wooden sticks instead of dice, and shamans in Madagascar used seeds cast on a circle. In all these instances of "casting lots" to determine the outcome of a specific question, people believed that the gods manipulated them to illustrate Divine will.

Doctrine of Signatures

Paracelsus, a Swiss-born physician and alchemist of the 16th century, popularized the idea that God marked things of the natural world with specific clues of their intended uses. The outward shape and color of every living thing acts as a key to its inward virtue. Therefore, in considering the components for your wishcraft, don't overlook the power of symbolism. Choose ingredients that somehow represent your completed goal or progress toward its manifestation.

During the casting of a wish, the components should be treated as if the wish were coming to fruition. For example, if you are wishing for improved finances, secure a small bundle of dollar bills above your head, then let them "rain" down upon you. This way, the visual and subconscious effect is literally that of raining prosperity.

Dog

In the 1920s in Oxford, the sighting of a Dalmatian dog was considered good luck. As soon as it was seen, people crossed their fingers and made a wish. This may have originated with the early Christian symbology of the dog as a faithful, watchful companion who could drive away the devil (see also *Crossing fingers*).

If you have recently made a wish and a yellow dog or a stray dog follows in your tracks, it is a positive sign.

Dogwood

(see also *Trees, Flowers*)

Place dogwood sap on a handkerchief on Midsummer's Eve and carry this with you until your wish manifests (see *Summer Solstice*). Or pick a dogwood flower at midnight on Midsummer's Eve. As you do, whisper your wish to the spirit of the plant. Your wish will be fulfilled by the following year, if it is meant to be.

Dough

(see also *Bread*)

In Egypt, lumps of dough placed out on the night the Nile's waters begin to recede after a flood represent a wish for long life. One is made for each family member, and if they are found cracked by morning, the wish will come true.

This is similar to other types of dough and clay divination wherein each piece represents a person or wish. The piece to rise first, or to sink first when placed in water, is positively indicated. In particular, this system was used to uncover the name of a thief.

Driftwood

As a child, my grandfather told me to write my wishes on driftwood, then toss it over my left shoulder back into the sea. He said the waves would transport the wishes toward my goal. This particular tradition combines the Druidic reverence toward trees with the elemental power of water (see also *Trees, Water, Wells*).

In a Japanese legend, a poem was written on scraps of driftwood and set afloat by *Yasuyroi*, a political captive, with a wish that his mother might find the poem, know he was alive, and be comforted. An old priest and friend of the family did find the driftwood poem and delivered them to Yasuryroi's mother.

Drums

(see also *Flute, Bell*)

The Lapps used specially painted and ornamented drums as part of divination rituals when they wished to learn the future of a hunting expedition or the condition of someone's health. The drum was covered with reindeer skin, with bones and brass rings hanging from the sides. The shaman struck the skin with a rabbit's foot to tune in to the spirit world. The shaman was then able to act as an oracle.

Similar to this, the Scandinavians had what was called a runic drum (*rune bomme*) or fortune-telling drum (*Spa-trumma*). This may be the source of the early Victorians using a tambourine as part of their seance kit! For our purposes, one might chose to use a drum to focus awareness for wishing, especially those efforts centering around obtaining prophetic insight, communing with spirits and health.

Certain Hindu philosophies believe that the cosmos was drummed into existence, which is why *Shiva*, the god of both creation and destruction, is always portrayed as dancing.

Easter
· · · · ·

If you wear three new items of clothing on Easter morning it will help to fulfill your wishes and ensure good luck throughout the rest of the year (see also *Clothing*). This belief predates Christianity, when Easter was a celebration welcoming Spring and fertility back to the earth. It may also be associated with the number three, whose magical power was first expressed through the triune goddess as Maiden, Mother, and Crone, and later realized in the Christian belief in the Holy Trinity.

Russians exchange eggs and toasts with friends on Easter, wishing for their continued good health (see also *Eggs*, *Toasts*). Eggs are symbolic of life's renewal, which is why they are featured in many Easter traditions.

Eggs
· · · ·

The person who eats the first egg laid by a brown hen will get their wish. If this occurs on Easter day, they receive three wishes instead of one. The egg shell should be retained as a charm for continued good fortune.

If a pregnant woman wishes to know the sex of her unborn child, she can try the old Roman form of divination known as *ooscopy* or *oomantia*. For this, a fertilized egg is kept close to the woman's breast until hatched. The sex of the chick indicates the sex of the baby.

In old Russia, colored eggs were exchanged between couples with a kiss if they wished to inspire or rekindle love.

Emerald

If you wish for answers, especially to questions of love, communication, and discerning truth, try using an emerald as a component, as recommended by the old *grimoires* or folk wisdom collections of Europe. This may have originated from the claim of an ancient myth that the emerald came from the nest of a *griffin*, a creature which is part eagle and part lion. The eagle improves vision or awareness, and the lion strength. An easier alternative may be using an emerald-colored cloth, candle, or token.

Eromancy

(see also *Bottle*)

Practiced widely as a form of divination in Persia, the seeker takes a vase filled with water outside the home, then whispers wishes into the vase. If the surface of the water produces bubbles, this means the desires will be fulfilled. Some people in this region believe the bubbles are caused by a spirit or jinni (see also *Coffee, Jinni, Lantern*).

Eve of 12th Day

In Italy, on the eve of the 12th day of Christmas, Befana, the patroness of children, is said to fulfill wishes by filling stockings with gifts like Santa Claus. *Befana* in Italian means epiphany, and she is considered a cross between a witch and a fairy.

Evergreens

(see also *Trees*, *Incense*)

Druidic peoples decorated their homes with evergreens as an invitation for the sylvan spirits to take shelter inside from the cold. This act of hospitality ensured the family of better health and sustenance until spring. Evergreens were so revered because they stayed green throughout harsh winter months when all else seemed to die.

Evergreen branches make lovely, aromatic household decorations, and the dry needles are a good component for wishing incense, especially for providence and health.

Eyelash

(see also *Fingernails*, *Hair*)

In England, it is a common custom when an eyelash falls out to place it on the back of the hand, tip of the finger, or end of the nose, and blow upon it while wishing. If the eyelash falls off, releasing the energy, the wish will be fulfilled.

In early belief systems, things of the body like fingernails, hair, and eyelashes could be used in wishing for boon or bane. Later, this practice waned, and the tradition of wishing endured as a remnant of those beliefs. For modern wishing, a lost eyelash might be best added to a power pouch or other portable charm.

Fairies

Various fairy myths suggest that if you can capture a fairy or please it with special gifts, wishes may be granted in return. Granting the wish becomes a bribe to secure release or a whimsical expression of gratitude.

To contact the fey for wishcraft, look to plants and herbs frequently associated with them like foxglove and thyme. Watch for natural circles of stones, trees, or flowers. These are natural markers for fairy hills.

Fairy stones

Twin staurolite crystals or fairy stones shaped in the form of a cross encourage Divine favor and help to manifest wishes. In the runic language of the Northern Traditions, this is represented by the shape of *Gyfu*, which means quite literally "gift of the gods."

Feather

(see also *Birds*)

In ancient Greece, finding a grey and white feather portended that your heartfelt desire would come true. Try using feathers of this color as an all-purpose component in wishing, particularly as amulets or parts of wish pouches. Additionally, feathers float nicely on the winds helping to carry your power toward its goal.

Feldspar

If you hope to contact or see fairies, use a piece of feldspar in your wishcraft. This is said to attract them along with thyme and wood shards from thorn, ash, or oak trees. Conversely, to keep mischievous fairies away, particularly the jinn of Arabic lore, use loadstone or iron in your magic (see also *Fairies, Jinn*).

In ancient Egypt, feldspar was used to inscribe the 27th chapter of the *Book of the Dead*, in the belief that the god invoked with the text would be pleased by the precious substance used to write his words. With this in mind, feldspar is a good option for wishes of divine blessing and assistance.

Fern

In Europe, especially renaissance England, the fern was regarded as a protective amulet. If found "flowering" (producing fertile fronds that resemble a flower spray) at midnight on St. John's Eve, anyone who gathers its leaflets may make a wish for treasures. By holding it in your hands, like a dowsing rod, any hidden treasure in the area will be revealed, and you will pass through the region without a trace (see also *Ax*).

Additionally, those who carry the minute spores of ferns, formerly believed to be seeds, increase their luck and the sometimes whimsical operations of serendipity in their lives.

In English folklore, the mischievous spirit Puck appears among ferns at midnight to grant anyone who sees him a wish for fortune, like a purse filled with gold.

Festival of Sarasvati

Among Hindus, Sarasvati is the goddess of learning and wisdom. On her festival day, January 12, children often come to Sarasvati's temples wearing saffron-colored robes, carrying a marigold, her sacred flower. The flower is offered to the goddess' image while wishes are made for help in the child's studies.

Fig leaf

(see also *Leaf*)

If your wish pertains to spiritual enlightenment, write this request on a fig leaf. If the leaf dries slowly, your wish will come true. This belief may have originated from the legend that claims Buddha reached enlightenment while sitting beneath a fig tree.

Fingers

(see also *Crossing fingers*)

Cross your fingers while making your wish. This hopeful gesture encourages good luck. The pagan use of the cross as a talisman dates back to ancient times, when the equidistant cross was believed to be imbued with the powers of the four elements.

Fire

(see also *Pyromancy*)

On May 3rd in ancient Rome, people jumped over small fire pits while making simple wishes. This was part of the celebration known as *Bon Dea*, honoring the Roman Goddess of blessings. May 3rd is therefore an excellent day for any wishing.

Instead of a fire pit, consider leaping over a candle. As you cross from one side to the other, it marks a desired transition in your life. Remember to keep your goal firmly in your mind while you jump.

Another popular form of wishing in Europe involved tossing a piece of paper inscribed with one's wish upon the hearth fire, frequently on special occasions. If the paper was drawn up the chimney, the wish would come true. This custom may have grown out of early beliefs about the hearth fire as the "heart" of a home, symbolizing love and family unity.

In Portugal, young people wishing for love and health jump over fires on Midsummer's Eve after drinking from seven springs (see also *Numbers*). Similarly, lovers in Hungary jump over fires on this day to express their wish for their lives to be united (see also *Summer Solstice*).

Firsts

In Wales it is traditional to make a wish any time you have the first seasonal taste of any type of food, or when you pick the first seasonal flower. In other regions, it is common to wish on anything new, like the first robin sighted in spring, or the first vegetable harvested from the garden. In order for the wish to come true, it must be kept totally secret.

First visit

In Scotland, when you first visit another's home and your foot crosses the threshold, you can make a wish. This was actually a way that women in the Highlands helped break the ice with their guests. It also has some connection with the old tradition of bringing a small gift when coming to someone's home for the first time, which helped appease the hearth gods who protected the family and home.

Fish

Two fish are given to newly married couples in China as a wish that their physical union will be joyful (see Aero in the bibliography). This could be adapted by serving fish at the reception, making an ice-fish sculpture for decoration, or giving the newlyweds some type of fish knick-knack as a gift.

When eating fish, proceed from head to tail for good luck.

Fish have regularly been associated with divine figures, including the deity Oannes in Babylonia and Jesus Christ.

Flags

If made from a natural material, and marked with an emblem indicating your goal, flags can become a useful component for wishing. I suggest making the flag yourself to focus your energy, then flying it nearby to release your power on every wind.

In the Middle Ages and earlier, heraldic shields and banners announced families and clans to surrounding regions and peoples, much the way flags represent nations and states today. To capture someone's banner during war meant capturing their power and status. Our contemporary reverence for flags is a vestige of these times.

Flint

In Scotland and Ireland, flint arrowheads from prehistoric times are believed to be fairy weapons. If you unearth one, dust off the excess dirt and dip it in water and wish for good health. Drink the water to ensure your well-being.

Flowers

(see also names of individual flowers)

At sunrise pick a morning glory or other flower typically associated with the movement of the sun. Make a simple wish upon it as the sun peaks over the horizon. It is said that the wish should come true by sunset. This tradition stems from the idea that the sun is the messenger of divine favor and a mighty ally. Dawn symbolizes the sun's renewed power over darkness.

As late as the Victorian era in England, it was thought that wearing the flower associated with your birth month would help fulfill wishes and bring overall luck (see also *Birth stones*). Balinese children leave rosettes made from flowers in their local temple by the light of a full moon, then whisper their wishes to divine celestial beings.

In Portugal, people gather different types of flowers on Ascension Day depending on what they wish for in the coming year. If they desire prosperity, they gather daisies. For peace, they gather poppies. In Japan iris petals are part of the traditional *Feast of Banners*, which takes place in early May. Here, family baths are dotted with irises to symbolize wishes for strength and courage, especially for any male child.

Among the Chinese, people gather outside on the night of September 8th for the festival of the Moon's Birthday. If a woman sees a "flower" fall from the moon (i.e., a meteor or falling star), she may wish for luck and fertility; a man may wish for prosperity.

Each of these traditions certainly have some animistic characteristics, but you can't help believing that the beauty of flowers has also contributed greatly to their use in magic and religion. They seem to reflect the radiance of the Creator.

Flowers, language of

In the Victorian Era, flowers were used in a symbolic language, often by star-crossed lovers, to express sentiments considered too risqué for plain speech. In the process of developing this colorful repartee, people also provided a symbolic tool for wishing.

In adding flowers to your wishcraft, consider the following brief list of correspondences from the language of flowers to decide what would be appropriate for your incense, potpourri, decorations, anointing oils, foods and/or beverages. Please note that this is not limited to flowers, but includes plants as well. More comprehensive lists of correspondences are available.

Benevolence, Compassion:	Potato, Elder, Allspice
Courage:	Thyme, Poplar
Energy, Power:	Lemon, House leek, Chamomile
Friendship:	Periwinkle
Healing:	Balm

Hope:	Hawthorn
Hospitality:	Oak and Holly (mixed)
Love, maternal:	Moss
Love, general:	Myrtle, Rose, Ambrosia
Muse, Originality:	Angelica, Sweet Briar
Peace, Rest:	Olive, Hazel
Pride, Self respect:	Carnation
Prosperity, Abundance:	Cabbage, Wheat, King Cups
Strength, Vigor:	Fennel, Cedar
Victory, Success:	Palm
Virtue:	Blue Violet, Mint
Wisdom:	Mulberry

Flowers, red

(see also *Colors*)

In Hindustan, a region of northern India, wreaths of a red flower known as *Ag* are placed on images of the god Sanee while wishes are recited. These flowers invoke Sanee's favor.

Flute

(see also *Drums, Bells*)

In India, flutes are used to charm animals, especially snakes. Hippocrates wrote about a man named Nicanor who fainted from the beautiful sound of the flute. Play flute music when performing wishcraft to build charisma and attraction.

Forked branches

According to the *Encyclopedia of the Occult*, specially chosen forked branches, called wishing rods, are used for divination in Germany. This practice dates back to ancient Rome where Cicero and Tacitus both describe the existence of *virgula divina*, or divining twig. To find something like water or a rich mineral deposit, the diviner holds the stick parallel to the ground and walks, watching for it to dip down, indicating the spot to dig. Robert Boyle, the "father" of chemistry, wrote in 1663 that the favored wood for wishing rods was hazel (see also *Hazel*).

In modern wishing, small forked twigs may act as a component in locating spells.

Fountains

(see also *Wells*, *Coins*)

Old Scottish custom has it that you will have more success with wishes made at a fountain if you approach it from the east, then move around it clockwise before making your wish. This follows the sun's movement and probably stems from solar worship. If you toss a coin into the fountain and it lands face up, this is a most propitious sign for your wish's manifestation.

Garlic

The ancient Greeks and Turks used garlic as a protective amulet to avert the evil eye or other curses because of its potent odor. Romans planted it at a crossroads as an offering to Hecate. Victorian women often braided garlic buds into wreaths for hanging in their pantry. The twining bound the power of the garlic into the decoration, then each time a bud was cut free, it released a protective wish (see also *Knots*). Garlic continues to be an excellent ingredient in wishing for health or safety.

Garnet

According to a 13th century text by Ragiel entitled *The Book of Wings*, the garnet, a form of silicate, is a good component for wishes focused on health, honor, and safety in travel, especially if engraved with the image of a lion.

Garter

A woman wishing to bear children should wear a garter of straw or shells, preferably on her wedding day.

Ginseng

Legend has it that at night the ginseng plant grows and rises from the ground. Whoever witnesses this is granted a wish.

You can also carve representations of your wish into a whole Ginseng root. Toss this in running water to convey that energy where it's needed. Ginseng may have gained this reputation due to its healthful qualities as a natural tonic.

Glogg

(see also *Wine*, *Wassail*)

Glogg is a Scandinavian yuletide beverage made from wine, spirits, and various spices. When given the honor of providing the first toast of this beverage, it is traditional to make a wish of health for all those gathered. By so doing, you and everyone within hearing range are ensured of well-being throughout the coming year. This tradition is akin to that surrounding wassail.

Gold

(see also *Coins, Sun*)

If you are wishing for improved goodwill and influence with others, carry a circular piece of polished gold engraved with a pentagram. This talisman of the sun is recommended by A. E. Waite, co-creator of the Rider-Waite Tarot Deck®. To improve this talisman's effectiveness, construct it when the moon is in Leo, and bless it with incense of cinnamon, saffron, sandalwood, laurel, and heliotrope. Once completed, carry it in a yellow silk pouch.

In old European folklore, the best way to gain wishes from a leprechaun was to find his pot of gold and hold it for ransom. However, since a leprechaun is a type of fairy, your wish may be granted in a humorous or indirect manner (see also *Fairies*).

Good Friday

(see also *Days*)

When the clock strikes three on Good Friday, make a wish in the form of a prayer and it will be granted. The timing of this wish probably comes from the Christian image of God as triune (Father, Son, and Holy Spirit), and the importance of this day on the Christian calendar.

Goose

(see also *Birds*)

Give a gift of food to the needy—especially a goose—on St. Martin's Day, November 11th, to gain a wish. St. Martin was known for acts of charity like giving his cloak to a cold beggar. Once when hiding from pursuers a goose cackled and betrayed Martin's hiding spot. In requital, the goose is "cooked" today.

If a goose flies overhead soon after you've made a wish, it is a propitious sign of its fulfillment.

Gooseberries

During the 16th and 17th centuries in Britain, those wishing for wisdom would eat gooseberries on Whitsunday. Ale might also be added for improved luck.

Grains of paradise

Take a handful of grains of paradise. Toss them in a circle clockwise, beginning in the east, while focusing on your wish. This is most helpful for wishes involving love, prosperity, passion, and good fortune.

Grass

Write a wish on a stone with grass, then bury it so the wish grows, or toss it in running water so the energy moves to where it's most needed.

Hold a long blade of grass in one hand. Wish fervently while you await the sound of a favorite bird singing. When you hear it, tie a knot in the blade of grass and leave it to grow with your hopes. This tradition is a variation on one from Indonesia used for fruitfulness (see also *Knots*).

Hair

(see also *Eyelash*)

On a child's birthday, take a lock of hair gathered when they were a newborn and wish upon it. Tie this with a flower and a special ribbon, then press the resulting charm into a book. Make the first wishes for health, beauty, intelligence, and luck! On the third, fifth, thirteenth, and seventeenth birthdays, add to the charm and keep it in a secret place. Give it to the person when they are twenty-eight with all the accumulated good wishes.

Hare

In some rural parts of England and Scotland, there is a tradition of making a wish when a hare passes by. The hare is strongly connected with Goddess and moon worship, so such a wish probably originated as a supplication to those powers (see also *Words*).

Hawthorn

Hawthorn is sometimes called the wishing bush. Make your wish while holding a piece of attractive cloth, then stick it on one of a hawthorn's thorns. This tradition may have developed from the old superstition that it is a sacred fairy plant. The fey would witness the wish-making, delight in the offering of the cloth and, if feeling generous, would help the wish manifest. An older association for hawthorn is that it was representative of the ancient maiden goddess, who was hopeful and auspicious.

In Turkey, people present a hawthorn branch to each other when they wish to receive a kiss.

Hay cart

Meeting a loaded hay cart coming toward you should be honored by a wish. To make this wish effective, you must make it when you first see the cart approaching and not look at the hay again. This belief stems from two sources. First, a loaded hay cart meant a good harvest for someone, so wishing on it was a way of trying to share in that good fortune. Also, hay carts often accompanied merchants, whose presence in any town was a welcome sight.

Consider adding small bits of hay to wishing incense and charms. Hay bales may also be used to portend the success or failure of your wish by placing two crossed arrows (preferably wooden but plastic is okay) directly into the top of the hay. If the arrows fall toward the right or forward, the omen is positive; to the left or backward is negative. If the arrows split apart this means some type of digression from goal of your wish, and together indicates unified energy for boon or bane.

Hazel

In Welsh tradition, wearing a woven crown of hazel when wishing helps manifest your desire. Hazel was a sacred Pagan tree symbolic of knowledge and fertility.

The Romans considered hazel a sign of authority. If your wish pertains to influence, control, or personal mastery, it makes a good central component.

Hazelnuts

Giving a bundle of hazelnuts to newlyweds was an old Victorian wish for fertility. Hazelnuts were also used in divining the outcomes of various actions including wishes. To try this yourself, place three nuts in a well-maintained fire. If they pop and burn brightly, your wish is starting to manifest. If they smolder or don't ignite, it wasn't meant to be.

Hematite

Pliny the Elder suggested wearing or carrying a hematite if one wished favorable judgments in court. He got this idea from a text written in 63 B.C.E. by Azchalias of Babylon who worked for King Mithridates the Great, an avid lover and collector of precious stones.

Holly

To make wishes come to fruition, gather nine holly leaves on a Friday night at midnight. Wrap them in a cloth with nine knots and sleep with the charm under your pillow for nine days. This charm may only be used once, then should be disposed of by burning or burial.

Honey

(see also *Bees*)

In India, honey is dripped on the tongue of a child* as a wish for a life of sweetness or words of wisdom. In this region, the gods Krishna, Vishnu, and Indra are called "born of nectar," and the love god Kama's bowstring was formed from cooperative bees.

In Egypt, honey was offered to the goddess Min when wishing for fertility. Egyptian legend has it that honey was born from the tears of Ra. The Greeks used honey regularly as a restorative, Aristotle himself likening the substance to the distilled dew of stars and rainbows. The Romans believed consuming honey could bring forth the muse. In European lore, honey was associated with mother goddesses including Artemis and Demeter.

Horse

If you meet a white horse, spit upon the ground, cross your fingers, and make a wish. If possible, make the wish before you see its tail. This particular wishing tradition shows vestiges of many beliefs. In fairy tales, the hero often rode a white horse, a symbol of purity. Horses were also sacred to the Celtic goddess Epona. The cross has symbolized both Christ and the four major elemental powers.

* Please note that it is not advisable to give honey to a child under the age of one.

Another version of this type of wish is performed on the hillsides in England where outlines of white horses were carved into the ground. In this case, one should stand between the eyes of the etched horse while making your wish to be certain of it coming true. In Berkshire, England, there is one such portrait which dates back to the victory of Ethelred and Alfred the Great over the Danes at Ashdown.

Horseshoes

During the Middle Ages, if you found a horseshoe, you hung in the home for protection against negative magic and for good fortune. This may have originated because of the old belief that a smith's power over iron was magical. An earlier source for this tradition comes from the Greeks who called this amulet *selene* after its moon-like shape, and associated it with lunar powers. People in India also used horseshoes to ward off evil spirits.

It is believed that hanging a horseshoe with its curved end down "catches" blessings, while the open end down "showers" luck on all those passing underneath.

To make a successful wish on a horseshoe, you must pull the shoe from the horse yourself. Then the wish must be made for someone else or it won't work.

Incense

(see also *Candles*, *Fire*)

The first incenses were highly aromatic gums and resins used for religious worship throughout the ancient world. Frequently, people would burn symbols of their hopes and prayers along with the incense believing that the smoke carried their wish to the gods.

Good components to use for wishing incense include dried dandelion tufts, bay leaf, sage, powdered beechwood, dogwood petals and violet. Add an herb or spice that mirrors the goal of your wish for improved focus. For example, if your wish pertains to love, add rose petals (see also *Dandelion, Bay, Sage, Beechwood, Dogwood, Violet, Rose*).

A friend sent this incense recipe: mix one tablespoon each of cinnamon, crushed bay leaf, and galangal. Add this to a cup of fine sawdust along with a few drops of vanilla extract. Finally, add a pinch of saltpeter if you don't want to use charcoal for burning.

Write your wish on a piece of paper, placing the incense on top. Lift the corners of the paper and twist them tightly to make a little paper sack. Light the wish sack, visualizing your wish as fulfilled. If the paper burns entirely, the wish will come true almost immediately. If you have to relight the paper once or twice, obstacles must be cleared before fulfillment comes. If you must relight the paper more than that, it is doubtful this wish is good for you. Reconsider your motivations before trying again.

Iron
· · · ·

(see also *Nails, Horseshoes*)

If you find a piece of iron on your path, pick it up, spit on it, and throw it over your left shoulder while making a wish. This belief is strongly linked with horseshoes and the magical powers ironsmiths were once believed to possess. According to folk superstition, throwing a good luck charm over the left side would assault malevolent spirits residing there, and prevent them from hindering a wish.

In *Occult Sciences*, A. E. Waite gives a formula for making a talisman out of iron for those wishing to be protected from their enemies. One side of the iron is inscribed with a lion in a *Seal of Solomon*, and the other bears the image of a sword in a pentagram. This should be made on a Tuesday when the moon is in Aries or Sagittarius (see also *Astrology*). Bless this using rue incense and then keep the charm in red silk.

Jacinth (Hyacinth)

(see also *Sapphire*)

Jacinth was a blue precious gem (possibly a sapphire) mentioned by Albertus Magnus in the 13th century and Pliny in A.D. 23. It was considered a sleeping aid. Additionally, they and others recommended this stone to those individuals who wished for protection from plagues and lightning or for safe travel, or to those longing to improve their personal honor, wealth, or wisdom. So powerful was this stone's reputation that even St. Hildegard, Abbess of Bingen in 1179, recommended it to dispel magic spells, specifically those that caused afflictions.

These days, jacinth is a semi-precious red-orange stone of the zircon family that is fairly inexpensive and easily obtainable for magical use. Check with your local New Age shop, lapidary, or geology department. Use it as a component in wishes for your health and welfare.

Jade

In China, if a groom wished for a long and successful marriage, he would present his fiancee with a jade butterfly. For Chinese, jade symbolizes longevity, and the butterfly is a symbol of love and marriage (see also *Butterfly*).

Jasper

Carry or wear jasper if you are wishing for improved mental ability or eloquent speech. Pliny and Magnus both recommended it for these purposes. During the fourth century it was considered a potent amulet against evil spirits, and in the Middle Ages jasper was called a "rain bringer."

Jet

During the 17th century in Spain, a cross of jet was worn by those wishing to rid themselves of "fascination"—the susceptibility to being charmed. John Lazarus Gutierrex recommends this use in the *Opusculum de Fascino*, written in 1653. For modern purposes, this stone might be advisable for bridling flights of fancy.

According to Pliny, if you wish to know if something is poisonous, place it in a jet cup. It is said this cup will cause any poisonous thing to hiss like fire. Or, if a jet stone is put in poisonous wine, half-circles like a rainbow will appear as a warning not to drink it.

Pliny also claimed that magicians tossed jet against a hot ax to determine the outcome of a wish. If the jet burned to consumption, this portended the wish's manifestation (see *Ax*).

Jet was also known as gargates, and Prussians called it black amber.

Jinn

In Persia, if one wishes to conjure a breeze, they are directed to call upon the Jinn known as *Bad* for aid. This evocation is most powerful on the 22nd of the month, the day over which he presides (see also *Coffee, Feldspar*).

For more information on contacting and working with such Beings, return to the section *Evoking Spirit Guides and Symbols* (p. 49).

Job's tears

(see also *Seeds*)

Toss seven "tears" into moving water while focusing on a wish, or carry them constantly until a wish is fulfilled. Job's tears specifically aid magic for health and serendipity, the number seven is for completion.

Kelp

Kelp is eaten on New Year's Day in Japan as a wish for joy (see also *New Year's Day*). Country lore from around the world tells us that if you wash your floors with kelp, prosperity will follow, especially for store keepers. Thus, kelp is a good addition to wishing incense specifically for financial improvements (see also *Incense*).

Kelp gained its favor in Eastern lands as a gift of the great Mother Ocean, from whom life sprang, and whose providence to such island communities was unquestioned.

Kephalonomancy

Kephalonomancy is a type of divination from Germanic tradition, in which people placed their hand on the head of a donkey when wishing to discover the name of a criminal. Names were then spoken to the donkey. When it brayed in response, that indicated guilt. Alternatively, a piece of carbon was lit and placed on the donkey's head. If the carbon crackled simultaneously with the speaking of a person's name, guilt was assumed.

In modern wishcraft, one might consider using the image of a donkey or some carbon paper as a component for spells in which you wish to discern the truth.

Kites

As a child, my friends and I would loosely tie small strips of cloth—symbols of our wishes—to the tails of our kites. If the strips came off while the kite was aloft, we believed it sent the wish on its way. I can't remember where this idea originated, but it certainly gave me many pleasurable days filled with hopeful musing.

To make this ritual even more meaningful to you, use scraps from old pieces of your clothing whose color or associated memories symbolize your goals (see also *Clothing*).

Knots
· · · · · ·

Early magic lore from many parts of the world including Scandinavia and Asia include knots, which symbolize the binding and releasing of specific energy. Knots were used in weather magic to avert sickness, as protective amulets (against evil spirits), mnemonic devices, and as symbols of love (as in "tying the knot").

In terms of wishing, knots have three basic uses. First, you can tie up anything that may impede your wish—or a symbol of it—in a knot, then bury or burn it to disperse the negative energy. This also works for wishes of banishment or ridding yourself of sickness or bad habits. With the second use, you bind something that symbolizes your wish in a knot, then at an appropriate time, based perhaps on astrological aspects, you release the item to free the magic. Thirdly, you can use knots to create tokens to carry with you until the wish comes true. For example, bind red, yellow, and blue strings together with three strands of your hair in three knots while stating your wish out loud three times. Wear this token in your hair or on your wrist, and when the wish manifests, burn the token with a prayer of thankfulness.

In addition to these uses, a friend recommends taking a cord as long as your body and tying one knot in it each day for nine days. Tie the first knot in the center, then tie successive knots on alternating sides for the remaining eight days. As you tie, recite this little rhyme

> By knot of one, my wish is spun
>
> by knot of two, my wish come true
>
> by knot of three, its form I see
>
> by knot of four, it grows some more
>
> by knot of five, it comes alive

by knot of six, this spell is fixed

by knot of seven, it reaches the heavens

by knot of eight, it speaks with fate

by knot of nine, what I want is mine!

Place the cord in a safe place. The wish should manifest in 21 days. If you do not like the results of the wish spell, untie the knots backward over nine days to dispel the magic.

Finally, you can use a singularly knotted piece of yarn much like a wishbone, according to one bit of lore. Two people tug on opposite ends of the yarn until it breaks, and the one to get the piece with the knot in it gets their wish.

Labyrinth

(see also *Symbols*)

In Baltic traditions, if one wished for fair weather and soft breezes they would build a stone labyrinth on the sea shore. The twisting and turning maze of the labyrinth held the magic and trapped the bad weather neatly within.

Ladders

If you walk under a ladder, stop for a moment, cross your fingers, and make a wish to avert bad luck.

Ladybug

When a ladybug lands on you, take it gently in hand, make a wish, then release it. The direction it flies indicates the region from which your good luck will come, or possibly a future mate. Wearing a pin or other jewelry that depicts a ladybug acts as a talisman to draw loving devotion into your life.

Lanterns

(see also *Candles*)

In the *Tales of the Arabian Nights*, rubbing a magic lamp with a jinni trapped inside would release the powerful entity from its imprisonment and earn the liberator three wishes. In your wishcraft, this may equate to polishing a lamp using clockwise strokes around a symbol of your goal. The slow, rhythmic, repeated movements will improve your focus on the wish. The clockwise movement draws positive energy, and the lamp itself is an emblem of light and hope. Another modern twist on this tradition involves dabbing scented oil on the bulb of an electric lantern, then turning it on to release the magic's energy. Most lamp switches turn clockwise, and the heat of the bulb releases the aromatic energy in the room for sympathy.

In Japan, it is customary to use a lantern during special festivals for the dead. The purpose is twofold. First, it acts as a sign of welcome to familial spirits, and secondly it represents a wish that the spirits find their way home safely from the hereafter.

Lavender

To know if your wish will come true, place a little lavender beneath your pillow. If you dream of the wish, it will come to pass. Additionally, herbalists such as Pliny the Elder and Nicholas Culpeper recommended the scent of lavender for decreasing anxiety and providing a more restful sleep.

The Greeks often burned lavender in their temples during midsummer rites to carry prayers to the gods (see *Summer Solstice*).

Leaf

· · · · ·

(see also *Trees*, *Hawthorn*)

On Halloween, if you can catch a leaf falling from a tree before it hits the ground you may make one wish. Similarly, if you catch a falling leaf at any other time in October, it is a sign of good luck and health through the winter. This belief has its origins in ancient tree worship and the symbolism of Halloween as the Celtic new year.

Leeks

· · · · · ·

In Greek tradition, leeks were one item used in the ancient pharmaceutical as a protective ingredient. Their pungent aroma was thought to scare away malevolent spirits.

The Welsh use leeks as part of their annual spring plowing cooperative known as Cymmortha. Each Welsh farmer contributes a leek for the community stew to show unity. As they drop the vegetable in the pot, each person makes a wish for the town or village. The hopes and wishes of the entire population are then "cooked" together.

This type of tradition might make a nice addition to family or group reunions as part of a potluck meal. Each attendee can bring something for the stew pot, and voice a wish for the group as they toss their contribution in. Eating the stew then internalizes the power of the magic.

Lilac

· · · · ·

(see also *Flowers*, *Clover*)

If you discover a five-petalled lilac, this is a powerful and rare good luck charm similar to a four-leaf clover. Pluck it while making a wish, thank the bush for its gift, and carry the token with you.

Lily

(see also *Flowers*)

Make a wish upon the first blossoming lily you see in spring. Lilies are a traditional symbol of purity and were also associated with the angel Gabriel, making them a potent supportive component for wishing (see also *Firsts*).

Lodestone

(see also *Feldspar*)

Orpheus, the mythic Thracian poet and musician, felt that those who wished to learn directly from the voice of the gods should have a lodestone. He also felt it would help its possessor commune with spirits and see the future. Other medieval folk healers credited lodestone with the power to cure wounds and headache because of its magnetic nature.

Use a lodestone in wishes to improve your reception of messages from the Higher Self or other universal powers. Alternatively, use it as a component in your spells for improved health, foresight, or luck.

Loy Krathong

Loy Krathong is a celebration that takes place on November 9th in Thailand, and it is a day for wish magic. Thai people make miniature offerings of banana leaf boats with candles, incense, flower petals, and coins in them. When the sun sets, everyone launches her or his boat with a wish. If the candle is still lit as the boat moves out of view, local custom says the wish will come true.

In the interest of protecting the environment, I suggest doing something like this using smaller boats or floating candles on an enclosed water surface, like a pool. Push your boat out on the water, and if the candle stays lit until it reaches the other side, it is symbolic of manifesting energy.

Marjoram

Plant marjoram in your garden if your wish pertains to increased wealth. Care for the plant tenaciously, however, for if it dies, prosperity will also wane (see Keller in the bibliography).

Marjoram can also be used as a component in love wishes, as it was sacred to Venus and Aphrodite.

May Day

(see also *Beltane*)

Here is a May Day ritual from a friend. Give each participant in your ritual circle a thirteen-inch length of ribbon. Instruct them to make nine wishes, tying one knot in the ribbon for each. When this is completed, two people in the circle tie their ribbons together, then pass them in a clockwise direction (for positive, manifesting energy). When the bundle finally returns to the first person, everyone gathers close to the ritual fire.

All hands should touch the knotted bundle, then toss it into the flame. While the ribbon burns, each person should visualize the wishes coming true. Chanting may be added until the flames die away to add power the rite.

May dew

(see also *Dew*)

In Scotland it is believed that young people who wash their faces in dew before sunrise on May Day will get their wishes, especially ones relating to love. May dew's power comes from the fertility symbolized by Beltane festivals and the welcome return of spring.

May pole

The May pole is a traditional centerpiece of May Day festivities, adorned with flowers and lengths of rope, which are held by the celebrants as they dance in a circle around the pole. A group in Texas weaves its wishes into the ropes of the May pole as they wind around it. Each wish is left to germinate through the spring and summer. Then, the ropes are unwound on All Hallow's Day to release the fertile energy for manifestation.

Meteor

Also often called a shooting star, it is customary to wish on these brief, bright, streaking lights before their beauty fades. Because such images are not overly common, people felt the meteor might actually be a spiritual presence of some sort, especially since it appears as a streak of white light.

Milk

(see also *Cream*)

If you wish to invite a watchful fairy to your home, leave fresh milk outside every evening as a gift. In Scotland, they believe this action brings the *Gruagach* or long-haired one, who is particularly protective of farmers and cattle herders. Other lore from this region indicates that sweet cream is favored by the Fey, and helps draw out those elemental energies. Use it on holidays when the fairy folk are most active: May Day, Lammas, and Halloween.

Cream has long been associated with the Mother aspect of the Goddess, which includes the things that we can only understand through intuition. Therefore, use milk and cream as libations or beverages in wishing for improved intuition.

Mince pies

There is an old English poem recounted in a *Dictionary of Superstitions* which goes, "Mince pies grant wishes, let each claim his prize, but as for us, we wish for more mince pies!" Some say that only the person receiving the first slice of mince pie may make a wish.

Mistletoe

(see also *Yule*)

When taking down the mistletoe after Yule, save a small sprig and carry it with you throughout the year. During the next Yule celebration, toss this sprig on the Yule log with a wish. If it burns steady with flame, your wish will come true before a year is out. Mistletoe was sacred to the Druids, specifically as a panacea.

Money

(see also *Coins*)

If you find a dollar bill dated the year you were born, make a wish, then fold the dollar inward toward you three times. This will bring more money your way. Finding such a bill may be difficult, since paper money is not dated every year and is destroyed when it gets tattered. You can use a silver dollar from your birth year, however, and tuck it into your wallet as an alternative.

Moon

(see also *New moon*)

If you catch a glance of the moon over your right shoulder, make a wish! This tradition may have originated in Rome where the worshippers of Diana would assemble in her temples at the first sign of a waxing crescent moon (see *New moon*).

In Northern European traditions, praying to a full moon on Monday was considered a good way to increase the chance of a wish's fulfillment. This originated because Monday was the "moon's day," sacred to the goddess, Mani.

Make a wish on the day of the full moon, and it should come to pass by the next full moon (approximately 29 days).

Moonstone

In India moonstone is sacred and particularly useful as a token for lovers. When given as a gift, moonstone bears wishes of good fortune and joy to a couple. Moonstone gained this reputation in part due to its luminescence, that makes it look like the shining face of the moon.

Nails

(see also *Iron*)

Finding iron nails, especially those from horseshoes, has been considered a very positive omen. Those found near a grey mare were doubly so. When you find one, pick it up, spit, make your wish, then toss the nail over your left shoulder and don't look back. Tossing it this way was considered a way to keep the devil or evil influences from hindering or corrupting the wish, the left side being the traditional side evil approaches from. Alternatively, you may bury the nail in the ground near your home, or drive it into the front door, to protect yourself and your family from witchcraft.

Necklace

(See also *Coins, Gold, Silver, Symbols*)

On occasion, friends have straightened the clasp on my necklace, which had circled around to run into the attached charm, and when finished, have instructed me to "make a wish." To this day I have not discovered exactly why this tradition exists or where it originates. I suspect however, that it has some relationship with the ancient reverence toward precious stones, metals, and the symbolism of the circle.

Needlework

(see also *Crochet*, *Knots*, *Numbers*)

While you crochet, embroider, or tat pillowcases, make a wish for rest, peace, and health on every seventh stitch. This wishing tradition comes from other symbology associated with knots and numbers.

New moon

(see also *Moon*)

It is an old Norman custom to make a wish when you first look at the new moon. According to tradition, this wish will come true before the close of the year. For the ancients, the waxing moon symbolized growth and progress, which is why bread and beer were often made during the waxing moon.

New Year's Day

There is a traditional Romanian belief that the heavens open briefly on January first, and that anyone who catches a glimpse of paradise on this day will have one wish fulfilled.

In Northern Europe, it was traditional to open one's door right after the stroke of midnight on New Year's to welcome wishes and good fortune into the house (see also *First visit*).

The New Year in every culture is generally a time to celebrate one's fortune and perform various rituals to keep bad luck away. These include activities like paying the bills and making restitution with one's friends and family so that the new year will be filled with prosperity and peace.

The folk traditions of many cultures say that one should eat or drink symbolic beverages, or be doing something that symbolizes their wishes for the new year. For example, eating shrimp acts as a wish for prosperity because it is a luxury food, while drinking tea might symbolize a wish for health and tranquillity.

Noodles
· · · · · · · ·
(see also *Pasta*)

On certain Taoist holidays, offerings of vermicelli-like noodles are placed upon altars with peaches as a wish for long life and immortality. This association developed because of the extra long length of the noodles, which symbolize many years of living.

Numbers and numerology
· ·

Numerology can aid your wishing in many ways. For example, in the section on oils, the number of ingredients were chosen to emphasize numerical associations (see also *Oils*). Similarly, the date on which you perform a wish spell, or the hour, can be chosen for their numeric significance to enhance sympathetic energies.

Use the number one for wishes pertaining to self and single-mindedness, and two for wishes of partnership or those for the conscious mind. Three is the number of the ancient Goddess and universal trinities, thus it energizes wishes for symmetry and spiritual awareness. Four is good for elemental or cyclical wishes such as those pertaining to fairies or birthdays, respectively. Five is a versatile number, six is protective and devoted, seven is the number of the moon and insight, eight is best for wishes focused on change or completion, nine is for service and compassion, and ten relates to spiritual law and following one's own intuitive senses.

Nutmeg

Nutmeg is an herb for increased success and good fortune. To increase its effectiveness, keep it together with quicksilver in a red cloth container, or string whole nutmeg together with tonka beans and star anise for a lucky wishing necklace.

Nuts

(see also *Hazelnuts*, *Pine nuts*)

If you find two nuts in one shell, old York County custom instructs to eat one, then toss the other over your head or left shoulder while wishing. Afterwards, for the wish to come true, you must speak to no one until you can answer "yes" to the inquiry. This is a type of sympathetic magic wherein your "yes" reaffirms the wish.

To discern if your wish will come true, Victorian folklore suggests that one silently think on the wish while holding a nut, then place the nut in the hearth fires. If the nut catches fire and flames up, it is a positive sign (see also *Fire*).

Nuts became magically important because of tree worship in ancient cultures. The fruit from any sacred tree would likely be regarded as a potent gift from the Divine spirit.

Oatmeal

To wish away skin problems, wash the affected areas with oatmeal and cream while saying "Cream to cream, my skin is clean." This particular wishing tradition is very interesting in that it combines a magical procedure with a scientific cosmetic one. On a purely physical level, this especially helps people with oily skin because of oatmeal's coarse cleansing action. An alternative is using oatmeal-based soap.

Oils

Many Priests and Priestesses of old used specially prepared anointing oils to bless worshipers or prepare themselves to meet with the Divine powers. Since wishcraft seeks the aid of Universal Energies to achieve its goals, anointing oneself, one's tools, or one's tokens when casting the wish is quite apt.

While commercial oils are available, I suggest you create your own, choosing the herbs according to your goals (see herbs listed by name). Use a base of one cup of warm, good quality olive or almond oil, then add one teaspoon full of each herb chosen. Let these steep in a dark bottle for several days until the scent becomes heady. If using flower petals, remove them as soon as they turn translucent and be careful not to include any leafy parts—this will ruin your scent. Here are some good blends:

For general wishing:
1 cup olive oil
1 tsp. dried apple peel
2 whole bay leaves
1 four leaf clover
1 tsp. nutmeg

For love:
1 cup almond oil
Petals from 2 roses
1 tsp. basil
3 chrysanthemum petals
1 tsp. marjoram

Notice that in these examples I have chosen five main ingredients, one for each point of the pentagram. Five is the number for sacred duties and provides for the most balanced results (see also *Numbers and numerology*). If desired, you can also prepare the oil at a special time that accentuates your wishing energies or the topic of your wish (see *Dawn, Days, Astrology*). When the oil is ready, take it outside at nightfall and watch for the first star to appear. As it does, make a silent wish to your personal deity to bless and empower the oil for wishing. Wear this as a personal perfume as well, to draw positive energy.

Onions

(see also *Garlic, Leeks*)

In Egypt, people smell freshly cut onions at dawn on March 27th (Smell the Breeze Day) while making a wish for luck. On other days of the year, they may hold an onion in one hand while taking oaths or making wishes.

Egyptians at one time believed that the onion was a symbol of the universe and eternity. They often hung them in sickrooms to overcome maladies. In Europe this belief was mirrored by people placing poultices of onion on the stomach or under the armpit of patients to draw out poison.

Onyx

For those wishing to avert unwanted passion or cool the ardent pursuit of a suitor, onyx is an excellent talisman. It might be even better if combined with an amethyst, a stone that regulates unruly natures (see also *Amethyst*).

Onyx has been used for a very long time for protection. The Gnostics included it among their amuletic stones. Persians wore onyx to safeguard themselves from the evil eye. And onyx was one of the twelve stones of Aaron's breastplate as described in the *Bible, Exodus 28, 17-20*.

Orchid

(see also *Flowers*)

For those wishing for improved passion or fertility, the orchid's flower and root rival the mandrake in power. The word for orchid in Greek literally means "testicles." Additionally, the plant falls under the dominion of Venus, the planet and goddess of love and beauty.

Pancakes

In Britain, anyone who manages to snatch some pancakes before eight P.M. on Shrove Tuesday is ensured of better luck. The timing of this magical meal had much to do with curfew in the Middle Ages. It also marked the time when the sun was usually set, thereby taking "light" from the sky, so the luck would be likewise gone.

A modern method of wishing with pancakes entails creating the pancake as a physical representation of your wish. Eating the pancake helps manifest your desire.

Pansy

(see also *Flowers*)

Make a wish while randomly picking a pansy petal. If the petal you've chosen has four lines, this is a sign that the wish is manifesting. This type of divinatory technique was popularized in the Victorian Era, when an entire language was devised to communicate feelings with flowers when words might be considered improper (see *Flowers, language of*).

Paper

To determine the outcome of your wish, write it on a piece of paper, then place the sheet face down on a flat, fire-proof surface. Ignite the paper. If it burns completely, your wish will be successful. If a fragment burns, your wish will come true, but only in part or not as you expected. If the paper will not burn, the wish will not manifest (see also *Candles, Fire, Pyromancy*).

In China, special pieces of red paper are prepared at local temples with wishes inscribed on them in gold ink. These are burned with sandalwood to release the wish and encourage good fortune.

This type of divinatory wishcraft illustrates remnants of two important attitudes in the ancient world. First is the respect that people had for the written word. Since literacy was quite rare, anyone with the ability to capture words on paper was thought to be able to capture and use their power as well. Consequently, as soon as papyrus became plentiful, it was used for written spellcraft. Second, and far older still, is the awe inspired by fire and its sacred use for religious and magical purposes.

You can also write your wish on a piece of paper and put it under your pillow for three nights. If you dream of the wish, it will come true.

Parentalia

Parentalia was a Roman festival honoring the dead. On February 13, people left offerings of roses, violets, and foods—including salt, wine, and flour—at grave sites. These gifts symbolized wishes for continued peace and joy for the dead. This holiday was also dedicated to making restitution to friends and family.

Parsley seed

Sow parsley seed on Good Friday at dawn with your wish for luck, and the wish will come true (see also *Dawn, Astrology*).

Pasta

(see also *Bread, Rice, Noodles*)

Some Italian cooks claim that you should make a wish before separating two ravioli stuck together. In Italy pasta is considered a blessed food associated with miracles, so when two pieces stick together it is a positive omen, especially for lovers.

From a magical perspective, two is the number of partnership and balance. If your wish pertains to either of these, then the sticky ravioli are a good sign. If more than two are stuck together, check a list of numerical symbolism to see what your food may be trying to tell you!

Buckwheat noodles are eaten in Japan as a wish for prosperity. They are often given as gifts to neighbors to extend friendship and wealth (see Spayde in the bibliography). I suspect such associations developed because pasta is easily and inexpensively made, and shares some of the magical correspondences of bread, another "staff of life."

More specific correlations for pasta depend on the fillings and additives used in preparation. Meat pasta is best for wishes for prosperity and providence. Cheese pastas are associated with love and health. And because of its Italian association with miracles, pasta might also be incorporated in wishes for seemingly impossible circumstances.

Pearls
· · · · · ·

The Greeks and Romans used pearls regularly as talismans against numerous evils. During the 12th century Pope Adrian followed this custom by wearing an amulet that included a pearl. He believed that it ensured the successful development of all positive virtues.

The concept that pearls were protective may have originated because of their white color, which symbolizes purity and is also emblematic of the Goddess. If you're wishing to bring specific virtues into your life, especially wisdom, add a pearl to the component list (an imitation one will function as an effective symbol).

Pewter
· · · · · · ·

(see also *Coins, Gold, Silver, Copper*)

If your wish pertains to improved socialization and increased benevolence or sympathy from others, A. E. Waite suggests making a pewter amulet (see his *Occult Sciences* in the bibliography). Inscribe this with a four-pointed crown inside a pentagram on one side, and a eagle in a six-pointed star on the other. Do this on a Thursday when the moon is in Libra (see *Astrology*). Bless the amulet with grains of paradise, saffron, oak, poplar and/or nutmeg, then keep it in blue silk.

Pine nuts

(see also *Nuts*)

Giving someone a handful of pine nuts symbolizes a wish for your friendship with them to grow. This might be a nice gesture within newly formed study groups and covens. For example, the leader could bless a handful of the nuts and present several to each member. Each member could in turn place one of these nuts into a communal container to symbolize unity of purpose, and eat another to internalize unity.

Pins

If your wish pertains to overcoming fear, put a pin in a collar of a jacket while expressing the wish. Leave it there. This effectively fastens the energy in place. Never use this pin in sewing, however, or it will no longer work as an amulet.

Alter this tradition a little by pinning various empowered charms or other objects that represent a specific wish you have to your jacket. Wear the charm until the wish manifests.

Piroghi

(see also *Pasta*)

In Russia, *piroghi* are broken over a celebrant's head by relatives on name day, the feast day of the saint after whom the celebrant is named. If the stuffing falls on them, the celebrant may make a wish that gold and silver will likewise fall into their lives.

Plowing Festival

In old China, on a day in early Spring, military officials left offerings of thirteen dishes to the gods. These offerings acted as a wish and supplication for a bountiful harvest. They included several types of grains, fruits, broth, meat, and wine.

To adopt this tradition, the concept of bounty may be applied to nearly any aspect of your life. Simply change your offerings to mirror your goals, and make sure they are earth-friendly.

Pomegranate

American folklore tells us to make a wish before eating a pomegranate.

The Greeks portrayed Zeus as holding a pomegranate, which could give the fruit some powerful associations, especially with weather magic. In Egypt they were so precious they were used as money, thereby linking pomegranates to prosperity. Finally, the redness of the seed is a symbol of blood, life, and health (see also *Seeds*).

Poppets

Figurines made out of clay, wax, or cloth, *poppets* were important in various types of ancient magic including wishing. Most people are familiar with the idea of using a voodoo doll as a focus for magical will. Voodoo tradition, however, is only one of many that relies on the powers of sympathy. The basic idea is that a symbol spiritually becomes what it represents through ritual purification and blessing. Thus, someone wishing for a life-mate might tie two representative images together in an embrace as part of their rite.

If the poppet is made out of wax, one may add a wick and burn the image daily until the wish manifests. Many old *grimoires* (collections of folk wisdom) suggest adding spit, personal blood, and written words to the poppet to improve its power. Once the wish comes true, the symbol should be ritually destroyed to prevent its improper use by someone else.

For simplicity, a make-shift poppet can be designed using a scrap of personal fabric cut in a 5" x 5" square and filled with herbs appropriate to your goal. Tie this up like a sachet, and keep it where the energy will do the most good. For example, if making an intimate wish, carry the sachet with you. When making a wish for your family, keep the sachet at home in the room where people spend most of their time. If your wish has to do with travel, put the sachet in a travel bag.

Poppy seed

(see also *Seeds*)

To determine if your wish will come true, throw some poppy seeds on burning coals into a fire. If the resulting smoke rises straight up, it is a positive omen. If the smoke just hangs in the air, the portent is a negative one. Should the smoke move off to the left or right, this means your wish will come true, but not exactly as anticipated or only after some delays (see also *Candles*, *Pyromancy*).

In Babylonia this form of libanomancy or divination by smoke was practiced, except cedar shavings were used in place of the poppy seeds.

Potatoes

If you eat new potatoes they will grant you one wish (see Maple in the bibliography).

Being a tuber, potatoes are associated with foundations and earth magic. The white spherical nature of this vegetable also associates it with lunar energy. Try combining potatoes with another item that helps define your wish. For example, to give a relationship stronger foundations, add a little rosemary.

Pub

In Scotland it is some people's tradition to spit on a table and make a wish the first time they visit a new pub. This bit of wish magic seems to combine the ancient veneration of bodily fluids with the power of "spirits".

Pyromancy

(see also *Fire*, *Candles*)

Pyromancy is the practice of determining the future by the observation of sacred fires. The ancient Greeks used it regularly. In some instances, specific woods were used, while in others, any sacrificial fire was considered adequate for scrying. Other ancient people also observed torch fires and candle flames. If you want to use pyromancy, here's a basic interpretive guide:

Fire: A vigorous, quickly consumed fire is a positive omen. Those that smolder, have no smoke, or burn silently in a pyramid shape are all considered negative omens.

Torches: Pyromancy using torches is called lampadomancy. Single flames and three pointed flames are very good signs. Bent flames and twin flames are negative signs.

Candles: A more modernized version of lampadomancy uses candles. High, dancing flames mean good energies abound. Low, weak flames or those that go out speak of inopportune timing. If a candle sends sparks out toward the direction you released your wish, it is a positive omen. Away from that direction indicates malfunctions or delays. Alternatively, light two small candles side by side, if the left one burns out first, it is a negative sign.

Quartz

(see also *Diamond*)

Ancient people carried quartz as an amulet if they wished to improve their alertness and energy. This was likely due to the stone's resemblance to a diamond.

Various forms of quartz will have different uses and effects in your wishing. Clear quartz is an all-purpose power stone, for example, while rosy quartz is better suited to matters of friendship, self-love, and romance.

Rainbows

(see *Bridge*, *Crossroads*)

It is difficult to know for certain where wishing on rainbows originated. Among the Iroquois and Hurons, the rainbow is the wife of Hino, the Thunder spirit. In Incan beliefs, Cuycha was the rainbow god. Among the Greeks the rainbow was feminine, named Iris, and in Africa, it was called the Rainbow Snake and regarded as a beneficent spirit. In these traditions, wishing on a rainbow may have been a form of worship or supplication.

According to the *New Larousse Encyclopedia of Mythology*, a rainbow marks the bridge between the gods and humankind in Teutonic culture. They call it *Bifrost*. In Indo-European ideology, this god corresponded to Janus, the gate keeper who watches the threshold between worlds. Thus, to the Teutons, wishing on rainbows might have been equated to praying for safe passage to the afterlife.

Generally speaking wishes are best made on a rainbow when it appears on your right side. Adapting this concept, try making yourself an altar cloth out of rainbow hues to place at your right side when performing wish spells. All the components of the spell can be laid out on this cloth in the order of their use. The design for this cloth can be fairly simple. Cut seven long strips of colored cloth appropriate to rainbow hues. Sew them together in order from top to bottom, then attach one solid square of cloth as backing to the whole thing. To accomplish this, lay right sides together and stitch around the rectangle, leaving a small opening to turn the cloth right side out. Then hand sew the final seam using seven or thirteen stitches if possible. Seven is the number of completion, thirteen the number of finished cycles.

Red Ochre

(see also *Clay*, *Blood*)

Red ochre, a clay consisting of heavy deposits of hematite or iron peroxide, has a deep red hue. During the Paleolithic period and for some time thereafter, it was used in burial rituals to attempt to bring the dead back to life, or to wish them a vibrant, happy afterlife.

Anthropologists speculate that this tradition stemmed from the fear and misunderstanding surrounding death among early humans. At that time, what made someone seem to sleep endlessly was a total mystery. Nonetheless, red ochre was chosen for its blood red coloring, in the hope that the spirit of the departed would be beneficent, and not vengeful.

For modern wishcraft, red ochre is a functional blood substitute.

Rice

(see also *Cake*, *Bread*, and *Pasta*)

In China, throwing rice at newlyweds represented a wish for luck, prosperity, health, and many children. This is where we get our modern custom. Similar practices were found in Greece and Rome where wheat or nuts were used instead.

Chinese farmers have a tradition of feeding their fruit trees rice on the Winter Solstice to wish them happiness (see *Yule*). They believe that nature is as deserving of joy as humankind!

The Japanese eat rice to wish for good fortune, frequently at their birthday celebrations like we eat cake (see Bauer in the bibliography). This is because in this area of the world, rice is a central component to all meals, similar to bread in other lands.

Rice bowls

In Chinese folklore there is a story about a magical rice bowl of wishes. It could grant one wish a year, two every other year, or three every three years. The young man who obtained this bowl wished for a home, wealth, and many books to read. After the three years passed, he went to make his next set of wishes, only to discover his brother wanted to use the bowl. The two argued over the prized possession and broke it, whereupon all that it had created disappeared. The brothers realized the price for greed, but they also realized one gift from the bowl could never be erased: knowledge.

Rice cakes

In Japan, rice cakes are left for deceased relatives as a wish that their spirit will find everlasting peace.

Ring

(see also *Symbols, Wedding ring*)

Take a ring that you wear regularly and place it in the nest of a swallow until the night of a full moon. At midnight, retrieve the ring and wear it to fulfill your heart's desire, especially if it has to do with love.

Rings have been used in magic throughout the ages because they are a perfect unbroken circle of precious metal, symbolizing the sun. Many folktales feature a wishing ring.

Robins

(see also *Birds*)

If you see a robin at the first light of dawn, a wish will soon be fulfilled. Robins are traditionally the harbinger of spring, meaning life and warmth are returning to the Earth. Therefore, seeing them is considered a positive sign.

Rocks

As a child, I skipped rocks over water with a wish. If the stone skipped an even number of times, it was a positive omen. An odd number of times meant the wish would not be fulfilled.

A European superstition claims that tossing rocks into a church or cemetery is an act of supplication to the spirits for aid in any matter, including wishes. For this, white stones seemed favored, but the color may be changed depending on a wish's intention.

Rose

(see also *Flowers*)

According to Z. Budapest in *Grandmother of Time*, floating a rose on moving water on the night of Summer Solstice carries a wish to the Goddess. If desired, you may change the type of flower to reflect the theme of your wish. For example, the rose would be for love, whereas a dandelion might symbolize a wish for foresight. Dandelion in the Victorian language of flowers means "ancient oracle."

Some cultures have also regarded flowers as an emblem of the soul, and the scent of flowers as indicative of a spirit. Consequently, flower petals have been used in numerous forms of magic depending on their astrological and metaphysical correlations.

Rowan

(see also *Trees, Leaf*)

Wands of rowan were placed on the doorways of Norse homes at every quarter of the year to encourage good luck and bring wishes into reality. The branches were replaced regularly to ensure the magic's freshness. This may owe its origins to a myth in which the god Thor was saved from an Underworld river by the branches of this tree.

Before making a wish, it is advantageous to rub yourself with rowan and vervain leaves. Or you can dry them and use them as part of wishing incense.

Ruby

In 1561, Sir John Mandeville wrote a lapidary treatise in which the ruby was noted as being able to dissipate negative "vapors" and reconcile disputes between people. This would make it a good component in wishes for forgiveness, restitution, and peace. If obtaining this stone proves too costly, there are some candles that include gemstone powder, or you can try using a ruby-colored cloth or candle instead.

Sacred places

(see also *Crossroads, Fountains, Wells*)

Generally speaking, any region with an especially positive aura or ambiance, any area with lay lines through it, or any place regarded as holy is also a good location for casting wishes and all forms of spellcraft. Here, one may commune with Universal Powers and whisper wishes directly to their ears.

Sage

(see also *Leaf*)

Wish on sage leaf, then place it on your pillow for three nights. If you dream of the wish coming true, it will. Similarly, if you write your wish for luck on a sage leaf, then sleep on it, your dreams will tell you if it will come to pass. If you do not dream, the sage is to be planted so the wish may grow. In both cases, folklore instructs that picking the leaf in spring, before the plant blossoms, provides the best results for the wish and for cooking, too.

If you're wishing for longevity, eat sage regularly. Ancients trusted in the life-giving properties of this herb. It is doubly effective if eaten during the month of May. Sage gets its name from a Latin term *Salvia*, meaning salvation, which shows the high regard in which this plant was held.

Sailors

In earlier days, seeing sailors in town meant a ship had arrived with much needed supplies, so this was a welcome sign of good fortune. Thus, if one touched or brushed a sailor's collar before they reboarded the ship, it was considered a good time to make a wish (see also *Touching*).

Saint Blasius Day

The people of villages in southern Europe celebrate this saint's kindly, healing nature on February 2nd. One tradition is that of giving blessed garlic, apples, salt, and chocolate to children and animals alike as a wish for divine blessings and protection from witchcraft. The garlic and salt here both have purgative, protective natures, while apples represent health and chocolate a sweet life.

Saint John's wort

If you wish for success in a new endeavor, gather the root of St. John's wort on St. John's Day and keep it in your house until the wish manifests. After the wish manifests, return the root to the earth with thankfulness.

Folklore claims that the blood red sap of this plant symbolizes the blood of St. John (see also *Blood*). Paracelsus used the description of this plant to illustrate his *Doctrine of Signatures,* basically stating that God imprinted nature with clues to its medicinal uses. Because St. John's wort has porous leaves, for example, he felt it should be used in treating skin conditions. The Doctrine of Signatures became a cornerstone of natural magic, some principal ideas of which still remain to this day, like those in color and aromatherapies.

Saki

(see also *Wine*)

In Japan, sharing a cup of saki (rice wine) with someone acts as a wish for a long, happy friendship between you. At the coming of the New Year, average citizens and monks alike offer saki on temple altars to both the gods and ancestral spirits. This offering proclaims a wish to these powers for continued blessings upon the home, family, and village.

Salt

Sprinkling salt on your doorway symbolizes a wish that unwelcome guests will soon leave. You can also put a pinch of pepper under the guest's chair. However, placing salt on each side of an entryway welcomes people and encourages prosperity especially for merchants.

Salt was valued thusly because of its preservative qualities. Romans so revered this substance that they used it to pay their soldiers, which is how we come by the phrase "worth their salt."

Sand

Go to a beach just before high tide with a small natural offering (like a flower, rice, or wine), a candle, and some sweet smelling incense. Light the candle and incense, then state your wish out loud as you bury your offering. Repeat the wish out loud a personally significant number of times, then blow out the candle and take it with you. Leave the beach without looking back, allowing the incoming tide to receive your gifts and transport the energy.

If you do not live near a beach, try using a child's Etch-a-Sketch™. Place the candle and incense on the table before you, lighting both. Focus all your attention on your wish, and draw a representation of it in the toy's view screen. Leave this undisturbed by the candle and incense until both go out. Bury the ashes and wax in rich soil, and shake clear the image on the screen to release the energy. Or, alternatively, keep the image safeguarded until the wish manifests.

Sandalwood

Write your wish on a sandalwood chip and burn it to release those wishes to the Divine (see also *Fire*, *Pyromancy*). Sandalwood has been a favorite base wood for aromatic religious incense. Sandalwood powder burns very evenly, and may be blended in homemade preparations with a variety of other herbs that enhance your wish's intention.

Sapphire

According to Bartolomaei Anglici, a late 15th century writer on stones and their properties, sapphire was adored by witches for "working wonders." If your wish centers on magical proficiency or spiritual growth, this might be a good stone to choose as a component. Additionally, consider it for wishcraft that attempts the miraculous. Like other expensive gemstones, anything that is the color of sapphire may act as a substitute.

Saturnalia

(see also *Christmas*, *Yule*)

Saturnalia was an ancient Roman festival held on, or around, December 17th. It was a celebration honoring the god Saturn who ruled over sowing. On this day, no business was transacted, and all personal arguments were put aside in favor of revelry.

Gifts were given during Saturnalia, just as in modern Yule celebrations. Roman custom dictated that tokens be made or selected so they reflected specific wishes for the recipient. For example, a gilded apple symbolized the hope for prosperity, joy, and health.

Sayonara gift

In the Japanese folk tale of Young Urashima, the underwater Princess Oto gave Urashima a special parting gift that was not to be opened. Instead, Urashima was instructed to carry it with him as a token of Oto's wish that Urashima return to live with her after visiting his parents. As with the story of Pandora's box, the instructions were carelessly ignored, and Princess Oto's wish was never fulfilled. The box held Urashima's youth for the three hundred years he'd stayed with her. Once opened, it could never be regained (see also *Spell boxes*, *Wish boxes*).

Scarab

In ancient Egypt, carrying a scarab inscribed with the icons of *ikht neb nefer* enabled wishes to come into reality. Roughly translated the icons mean "all good things." The scarab was an emblem of the rising sun, which to the Egyptians represented the promise of life after death and the great god Ra. Consequently, people used it regularly as an amulet for numerous goals.

Egyptians also apparently gave engraved scarabs as gifts to convey wishes to the recipient. Examples include one on display in the Metropolitan Museum of Art which is part of the Murch Collection. Its inscription reads roughly, "May Ra grant you a happy new year." (see Kunz in the bibliography)

Scrying

(see also *Ceroscopy*, *Dactylomancy*, *Eromancy*, *Fire*, *Pyromancy*)

Many ancient peoples used scrying or gazing to determine if a wish or event would manifest. One divination technique was that of observing the surface of a crystal ball setting against a black cloth. If white wisps appeared moving upward or to the right within the sphere, it was a positive sign. To the left and downward was negative, and swirling clouds indicated no answer was available at that moment.

Another method involved observing the flames of a candle. If the taper's flame danced high and happily while the seeker focused on their wish, this indicated good energy. If the candle flame split in two, the fulfillment of the wish depended on someone else or outside assistance. If it smoldered or went out, however, the wish was likely never to come true.

Seasons

As with other matters of timing (see also *Astrology*, *Dawn*), choosing the season in which you release a wish spell can be a symbolic component to your craft. Spring is a good season for wishes in general, being a hopeful time, upbeat and full of fertility. Summer is best for wishes that require extra energy for manifestation, or those that center on passion and drastic changes. Fall's wishes are those for providence, abundance, and harvesting the rewards of one's labors. Winter wishes center on health and peace.

Besides the season itself, each holiday or celebration within that season may offer opportunities for wish magic. Consider the wishing traditions you know, or those you can unearth in festival books as starting points (see *Bean Throwing Day, Easter, Festival of Sarasvati, Good Friday, Loy Krathong, May Day, New Year's Day, Summer Solstice, Yule*).

Secrecy

Many forms of wishing advocate secrecy as an essential element to success. Two that come immediately to mind are birthday wishes and those placed on falling stars. It seems that the power of the magic is diminished by talking of it, even as some medieval mages believed that teaching about magic would decrease its potency.

One suggestion, if you feel you must share your wish, whisper it to the earth, then plant a flowering seed. This way, your wish can grow to maturity, and the earth is great at keeping secrets!

Seeds

(see also *Apple seed, Dandelion, Grains of paradise, Poppy seed, Sunflower*)

Plant a wish with a seed to help it grow. For best results, choose the seed according to the type of wish you're making. Examples include planting lavender to ease sadness and sowing corn for providence.

Dried tomato seeds worn around the neck fulfill wishes for a life mate (especially for women). This may have developed from the folk name for the tomato, the "love apple" (see DeLys in the bibliography).

Plant one type of seed in twelve containers on the first day of a full moon. Mark each container with the name of a different month, and water them equally. The first to sprout indicates when your wish will be fulfilled.

In China, the married daughter of a family offers a dish of seed gruel to the Earth Goddess on March 8th as part of an annual ritual. This offering acts as a wish for a bountiful harvest.

Seeds have been used in wishing because they are so strongly associated with potentialities, increase, and evolution. Additionally, when planted, they provided a visual representation of the magic's working.

Shepherd's Crowns

Carrying or wearing a shepherd's crown, which is a type of fossil properly called Echinucorys, aids in wish fulfillment by drawing luck to the bearer.

Shoes

In England, it was customary to toss a shoe when anyone set out on a journey as part of a wish for luck and safety in travel.

It may well be that we get our modern aphorism "put your best foot forward" from this old tradition. Among the Scots, Irish, Chinese, Hebrews, and Palestinians, shoes symbolize fertility and luck.

If you lace someone else's shoes, make a wish and it will be granted. This tradition has some connection with the symbolism in knots and knot magic (see also *Knots*).

Silver

(see also *Coins, Copper, Gold*)

A. E. Waite in his *Occult Sciences* recommends the use of a silver talisman for those hoping for safe travels. This talisman should have a pentagram with a crescent moon on one side, and a chalice encircled by the Seal of Solomon on the other. For most potency, prepare your wish on a Monday when the moon is in Capricorn or Virgo, and bless the talisman with an incense of camphor or mugwort. Keep it in white silk and carry it with you when you journey from home.

In ancient Rome, it was commonly believed that someone who owned an image of Alexander the Great engraved in silver or gold had a better chance to have their wishes fulfilled. This type of monarch worship was not unusual. Many ancient leaders, including the pharaohs and European kings, were venerated as divine or as having a god-like status. That is how the phrase "divine rite" developed. Since these leaders had the favor of the gods, their image similarly was construed as having great power.

Another tradition from Old England and other parts of Europe was to bury a silver coin beneath the threshold of a house as a wish for prosperity. Since Bretons believed that the *Ankou* or death spirit waited under it to capture spirits, placing a coin there acted as an offering to keep the home's occupants safe.

Snake
· · · · · ·

In the Sabine Hills near Ancient Rome, people honor Santo Domenico on May 2 by draping the canopy over his image with as many snakes as can be gathered the night before. Santo Domenico was a Benedictine monk who had power over wolves, mad dogs, and snakes. In this tradition, the snakes represent a community wish for Santo Domenico's blessings on pastures, flocks, trees, and grains. The snake being a beneficent symbol here may date back to Hermes staff, which was entwined with snakes, and which later became the universal emblem for the healing profession.

Sneezing
· · · · · · · ·

Sneezing once portends that a wish is soon to manifest. It also indicates good luck.

Snowdrop

If one wishes to be safe and healthy, even during the worst winter weather, carry this blossom. This belief stems from a German legend in which the snowdrop offers snow its white coloration after other flowers refused to do so. In return, the snow allows the snowdrop to be sheltered all winter.

Soapstone carving

(see also *Stones*)

Wishing is aided by intent concentration on your goal. One type of art that helps with focus is carving (see *Artistic Wishing*). Soapstone is a particularly soft stone, allowing it to be easily fashioned into symbolic shapes that represent your goal. You do not have to be overly adept at carving for this to work well. Get some fine files and gently draw an emblem of your wish in the stone using the file like a pen tip. For example, carve a $ sign for financial improvement. Once the image is finished you should carry it as a charm until the wish manifests, then pass it on to someone else to share in the blessings.

Socks

(see also *Clothing*)

If you accidentally put your socks on inside out, or put on two differently colored socks, leave them that way and make a wish. For the wish to come true, the socks should be undisturbed until sundown.

Solomon's seal root

Cut this root in two with a knife, and it will reveal what appears to be Solomon's seal. Write your wish on it, then carry it, bury it, or toss it in running water. The idea behind this tradition is closely connected with the reverence given to Solomon's seal as a magical talisman, similar to the pentagram seen when one slices an apple through the center.

Spatula

According to *Quaint Customs and Manners In Japan*, homeowners hang a small spatula over their doorway for protection. This gets placed with a wish that no one within will ever go hungry from lack of rice. The wish then ensures a good rice harvest (see also *Corn, Bread*).

Speaking simultaneously

When two people say the same thing in unison, they should cross fingers and wish together. The customary procedure is to interlock the pinkie fingers of each person's right hand and make a silent wish while speaking each other's name (see also the section *Word Power for Wishing*, page 24).

Some traditions for this are far more complex, including taking turns reciting rhyming phrases, then saying in unison, "May your wish and my wish never be broken." In this instance it is very important to put the other person's wish first, as acts of kindness encourage the wish's fulfillment. The wish should manifest within 31 days.

Spell box

Place an object in a decorative box that symbolizes your wish, preferably in manifested form. Alternatively write a detailed note that speaks of your fulfilled wish. Surround this with your favorite wishing or lucky herbs, and place a silver coin on top. Close the box and put it in an easily seen location.

Each day until your wish manifests, place your hand on the box and repeat the wish. When it comes to pass, give the coin away to a good cause to say thanks, such as placing it in someone's expired parking meter (see also *Coins*).

Spider

If you find a small red spider on a piece of apparel, this portends the fulfillment of a wish, especially those for money. To be certain your wish manifests, carefully take the thread to which the spider is attached and swing it gently around your head clockwise three times. Then release the spider with thanks (see also *Clockwise movement*, *Numerology*). If the thread breaks before three revolutions the wish spell will not work as this breaks the energy.

Spit

Ancient people thought bodily fluids, notably blood and spit, were very powerful and symbolic of the human soul. Consequently, spitting figured into many types of magic, and is found as a regular element of wishcraft. Examples of this can be seen under the headings of *Chimney sweep*, *Coal*, *Horses*, and *Nails*, to name a few.

Starflower

(see also *Flowers*, *Daisies*)

In France and Italy, these flowers were used for divination much like Americans use the daisy. However, the name of this flower (being designated as a "star") may make it even more useful in wishing if you recite your wish upon the first one you see.

Other flowers employed similarly were the marguerite and the poppy. In truth, I believe many flowers have been plucked by hopeful wishers, or those wanting to know the future, depending on what was readily available to them.

Stars

· · · · ·

(see also *Astrology, Moon*)

Wishing on the first star appearing or on falling stars may have developed from nature worship (see Introduction), in which animistic people believed that such objects had indwelling spirits. In Malay, if you wish for love on the first star that appears closely to the moon, a wedding will be forthcoming.

In Europe a slight variation on first-star wishing is to count nine stars each of nine nights, then make a wish (see *Numbers*). Magically speaking, nine is the number of completion. And most people know the old children's rhyme to recite when the first star breaks the darkness of a night sky (see also *Words*):

> *Star Light, Star Bright*
> *first star I see tonight*
> *wish I may, wish I might*
> *have the wish, I wish tonight*

If you see a falling star and wish for money, say the word "money" three times before the star disappears, and your wish will come true. Lovers who wish together upon a shooting star will receive health, and prosperity. If a star falls to your right, make a wish before it falls out of sight.

Stars are a good all-purpose wishing tool, but consider enhancing them by using other symbols. For example, if you see a falling star in spring, a wish for prosperity, fertility, or growth might be best (see also *Seasons*). Similarly, if the first star you see appears in the eastern part of the sky it might be combined with wishes for new beginnings and hope, since this is the region in which the sun rises (see also *Dawn, Days*).

Make a wish on the first star appearing while brushing a horse's mane. Then braid three stands of horse hair with clover and your own hair as a charm to ensure blessings. Keep this charm over a hay loft (or perhaps alternatively, over your bed).

Upon the appearance of the third star in the night sky, make a wish with a piece of gold in your left hand and this will encourage its manifestation. In Sicily, a variation on this has you cross yourself to bless the wish instead of holding the gold. In Taos, the first star of the morning is wished upon with reverence similar to that with both the first and third evening stars.

Stones
· · · · · ·

(see also names of individual stones)

Variegated stones (possibly agates) found below the docks in Scotland give one wish each to the finder if made into jewelry. These tokens are considered to be blessed by St. Columbia, who also protects seafarers from drowning.

Alternatively, milk was left in a holey stone as an offering to the nature spirits to increase the winds. For this purpose, the holey stone should be placed toward the direction from which the wind is desired.

Summer Solstice
· · · · · · · · · · · · ·

Taking place on or around June 22nd, the Summer Solstice is a magically potent day for wishes. This is because the sun dances its highest in the sky, which in earlier times was a sign of Divine blessing (see also *Gold, Sun*).

On the Summer Solstice, five herbs are considered most magical: rue, roses, St. John's wort, vervain, and trefoil. Additionally, according to legend, twelve flowers blossom on this day: buttercup, marguerite, nettle, rattray grass, wild parsley, St. John's wort, clover, vervain, lady's slippers, rue, roses, and scarlet lychnis. Of them, if you choose the right one and pick it at dawn, your wishes will be granted and you'll have eternal bliss.

Sunflowers

(see also *Flowers*, *Seeds*)

Cut a sunflower before sunset and make a wish. If the wish is not too complicated, it will come true within twenty-four hours.

Gather sunflower seeds by a setting sun and eat them to have a wish granted by the next night. However, this wish must also be simple in nature.

Sunflowers have solar attributes in abundance including strength, energy, fire, and mental keenness. Cook the sunflower seeds with spicy solar herbs to increase the effect, or pick the seeds at noon, when the sun is most potent.

Symbols

There are many symbols that the ancients used to empower or motivate their magical energy. For wishcraft, specifically, the following symbols can be used as helpful components:

- Three interconnected circles. These represent space, matter, and energy or body, mind, and spirit, all of which have to be in balance for successful magic.
- Three radiating lines, sometimes within an equilateral triangle. This is a Druidic sigil representing divine manifestation and the generative force, called *Awen*.
- A labyrinth pattern consisting of seven or eleven lines, both of which portend completeness and fruitful efforts.
- A sun with sixteen rays, which invokes blessings and smooth progressions (see also *Sunflower, Summer Solstice*).
- Waxing lunar crescent, an emblem for orderly change that works within natural laws (see also *Moon*).
- A circle drawn round a picture or emblem of your wish, which encloses it in good luck. Circles appeared regularly in ancient beliefs as a symbol of the sun, a powerful ally.

Tarot

The Nine of Cups in the tarot is an excellent aid to wish magic (see also *Numbers*). Place this card in the center of your sacred space with symbols of your wish all around it. Add appropriately colored candles and incense like vervain and rowan blended together. Leave this undisturbed in a fire safe area until the wish manifests, replacing the candle as necessary. Save the wax remnants to remelt for future wish magic, and scatter the ashes to the winds.

Tea

Make a wish for a mate as you pour the last drops of tea from the pot into a cup. This is an old Pennsylvania Dutch tradition. It is even more powerful if you drink the tea when Venus becomes visible in the evening, as Venus was the Roman goddess of love (see also *Stars*).

Threes

(see also *Numbers*)

Numerous myths, including those of the jinns and the rice bowl speak of multiple wishes as having specific limits, three being the most frequently reoccurring number. In each case, one may not wish for extra wishes. More than likely this is to remind us not to get too greedy.

Tin

Among the Scots, pieces of tin were cut to represent a specific wish. Then the symbol was placed near St. Thenew's Well, usually tied onto a tree (see also *Fountains, Trees, Wells*). Frequently these wishes pertained to personal health. Often they took place on July 18th, Saint's Thenew's Day, or during early February, May, August, or

November, all of which have important magical quarter days (Candlemas, Beltane, Lammas, and Hallows, respectively).

To adapt this idea, you may instead take your crafted piece of tin with your wishes to any water source at any appropriate time noted above. Take care, however, that the tin doesn't have any sharp edges to harm wildlife, especially birds that might be attracted to its shiny surface.

Toasts

(see also *Glogg, Wassail*)

Originally, to toast someone was actually a means of wishing them good fortune and health, and is still quite functional for this purpose today. Similarly, clinking glasses together was a way to scare off evil spirits. The marriage glass is broken after Jewish weddings for the same reason, and to symbolize the consummation of the marriage.

In some regions, the tradition of raising glasses together, however, comes from more of a political source than a superstitious one. When the Danish conquered the British Isles, people could not imbibe without the ruler's permission. Danes lifting their glasses signaled their approval for others to drink.

Tomatoes

In Italian homes, the tomato is nearly a sacred fruit. Place one on your mantle with a wish for prosperity, or on the window sill to protect the home (see also *Pasta*). If your hopes center on health, make tomato sauce and consume it! Finally, if luck is what you desire, find a tomato pincushion to keep with other special household trinkets. Use this pin cushion whenever you're making or repairing magical garb to release its energy (by taking the pins from the base).

Tonka beans

(see also *Beans*)

Similar to other items, tonka beans help manifest your wishes if you toss them in running water.

These may also be easily added into wishing pouches or sachets thanks to their size. Dye the beans an appropriate color for your wish by soaking them in warm water and food coloring.

Topaz

(see also *Chrysolite*)

If you're wishing to make more friends or increase your sociability, wear or carry topaz regularly.

Touch

Using the law of "like attracts like" as a guide, many people in earlier times believed that one could manifest a wish simply by touching something that resembled that desire. For example, touching the cuff of a wealthy person to improve prosperity, or the collar of a sailor if one wished to travel (see also *Boat festival*).

Applying this, keep an item that resembles your manifested wish in your spellcasting area, and touch it when you release the magic to direct the energy where it needs to go.

Trees

(see also *Leaf* and names of individual trees)

Vishnu, the Hindu preserver god, appeared in an incarnation as a tortoise that came from the bottom of the sea. As he appeared,

Vishnu bore the Elixir of Immortality, the moon, the Cow of Plenty, and the Tree of Wishes, similar to the Tree of Life in Western myths.

In Europe, trees were used frequently for wishes pertaining to health and happiness. For example, people wishing to rid themselves of sickness would tie scraps of their garment to a bush or tree to "bind" the illness to it (see also *Clothing*). Or at a wedding, people might place brightly colored ribbon into a tree to represent their good wishes for the couple.

Trickery

There are many folktales in which a mischievous spirit is tricked into giving clever mortals their wishes. For example, someone fast enough and ingenious enough to capture a leprechaun is granted their wishes for gold or other treasures (see also *Buckthorn*, *Fairies*).

In Swedish folk stories, a crafty sailor manages to trick the devil out of two perfectly good wishes by promising himself to service should the devil not be able to grant the third. The first two wishes were for all the tobacco and schnapps in the world. The third was for a drink of schnapps from the devil's stores. Needless to say, the devil lost another soul that day!

Turkey

(see also *Birds*, *Feather*)

In southern Mexico some tribal societies use a stuffed, dressed turkey as a wish token for peace for departed souls. In this way it is shared both as an offering and a feast for the bereaved family to ease grief. Comparably, in American Indian lore this bird is called "give away" to symbolize a giving spirit that cares for others.

The tradition of wishing on the turkey's clavicular bone, which is pulled apart by two people holding opposite ends, most likely started with fowl divination (a type of ornithomancy). This entailed letting the creature eat from piles of grain on the floor, then sacrificing the hen to the gods. After this, the "wish bone" was dried and two people who sought answers to their questions snapped the bone. The one receiving the longest side got the information provided to the diviner earlier in the proceedings. In this manner, we have come by the expression "lucky break," and the tradition of wishing on turkey or chicken clavicle bones.

The turkey is a bird representative of prosperity and providence. The Aztecs offered the Spaniards a meal of turkey by way of friendship, so this bird is useful in wishes pertaining to companionship, opening lines of communication, and hospitality. It is also a food representing thankful hearts, which positively aids any magic.

Turquoise

This stone is best applied as a component in wishing for protection. It is said to avert accidents and prevent weariness, but to work most effectively it should be received as a gift. In addition to this unique attribute, turquoise has all the same virtues of any other blue or blue-green stone (see also *Color*).

Vervain

In ancient Persia, Greece, and Germany vervain was an integral component in wish magic. It may be added to incense, sachets, anointing oils, baths, and potpourri for this purpose.

Vervain is especially suited to love, protection, peace, health, and prosperity wishes. For example, someone wishing to inspire love may mix rose petals with vervain gathered on Midsummer's Eve and drink a little in red wine. The remaining may then be mixed with oil to anoint the lips and bring passion with each kiss (see *Flowers, Summer Solstice*).

Another token for a married couple is made by binding vervain together with seven small sticks, St. John's wort, and snippets of hair from each partner. This should be bound gently together as a wish to keep love strong throughout the relationship.

Sprinkling your home with vervain water keeps malevolent spirits away. This tradition may have originated in ancient Rome where vervain was used to cleanse the altars of Jupiter.

Violets
· · · · · · ·
(see also *Flowers*, *Firsts*)

According to Victorian folklore, the first violet that blossoms in the spring, if found, grants the finder her or his dearest wish.

The violet, sacred to Venus, was the national flower of ancient Greece. In the Middle Ages it symbolized the twelfth hour of the day, a particularly magical time (see also *Dawn*).

Visions
· · · · · · ·
An ancient Persian book entitled *Oupnekhat* or *Book of the Secret* gives specific instructions to those who wish for inspired visions. To begin, one must sit on a four-cornered base, then close the gates of the body by plugging one's ears with the thumbs, closing one's eyes, holding the nose, and closing the lips. Then, all senses should be withdrawn into the center of one's being, seeking inner light. When the seeker can envision the heart flame—the Divine essence or Atma—and become one with that energy, she or he will deny worldly pleasures and attain visions.

Waking

(see also *Dawn*)

According to Hopi tradition, if you should wake exactly at dawn, the time when the sky first turns to dark blue instead of black, then when the sun appears you may ask a favor of it. Simple requests will be fulfilled by sundown.

Walnuts

(see also *Nuts*)

If you give a bag of walnuts to someone it becomes a symbol of a wish for their personal fulfillment. Because of the way walnuts appear, they also have strong associations with the brain and learning. Here knowledge is the magic that brings happiness.

Wands

In Australia, magical wands (or bones) are used in wish magic of the outback. People plant the energized wand in the earth, then speak their desire to it. Often this is in the form of a curse, but could be adapted for more positive ends. The stick is left in the ground for several days to send the wish through the land (see Maple in the bibliography).

In some of our fairy tales, wands also participate in helping make wishes come true. In the story of Snow White, for example, the fairy godmother wields her magic skillfully through a wand. Stories like this probably owe their origin to ancient Greek myths that discuss Bacchus carrying a wand of twined olive branches. When this wand touched humans, it endowed them with various beneficent qualities, including eloquence and ease of speaking, as with the consumption of wine. Mercury, the messenger of the gods, also carried a powerful wand (see also *Trees*).

Wassail

(see also *Glogg*, *Toasts*, *Christmas*, *Yule*)

Wassail derives from an Anglo Saxon term meaning, "be well." It is both a toast to someone's health and the hot, spiced beverage used for the toast. Wassail is usually served in a bowl at Christmastime.

Wassail may be easily prepared by taking a dry red wine and adding cloves, candied ginger, sliced oranges, a little lemon rind, cinnamon sticks, and brown sugar to taste. Warm these ingredients together with your wishes, then internalize them and stay cozy during the Yule season.

Water

To discover if your wish will be fulfilled, float a piece of bread, a leaf caught before it touched the ground, a flower petal, feather, or other light object on the surface of water (a lake or spring is best). Ask the waters if your wish will manifest. If the object sinks soon thereafter the answer is yes. This form of water divination was practiced in such diverse regions as Hawaii and Greece.

Wax, remnants

(see also *Candles*)

Save all your wax remnants from magical candles throughout the year. On Beltane, tie them up in colorful tissue paper with a bright purple ribbon (see *Colors*, *May Day*). Tie your wishes into that ribbon, then release the cache into the Balefire. As it burns, the positive magic from the rest of the year provides increased energy for manifestation (see also *Beltane*, *Fire*).

Wedding ring

(see also *Copper, Gold, Ring, Silver, Tin*)

When making a wish, turn your wedding ring around three times in a clockwise direction to help the wish come true. This superstition is connected to the belief that the vein in the ring finger connects to the heart, and therefore empowers your wish with love's strength. Additionally, the precious metals most wedding rings are made of helps the magic along.

Wells

(see also *Coins, Fountains*)

Wishing wells may have some connections to the ancient art of hydromancy, or divination by water. Practiced readily in Greece, Rome, and Germany, items like rings, stones, or gold were tossed or suspended in water and observations were noted. This too may have some roots in earlier animistic ideas, in which people saw wells as having an in-dwelling spirit that could be appeased. In *The Sacred Dance*, W. O. E. Oesterly writes, "Of course these superstitions often take the form of a belief that the sacred spring is the dwelling place of Beings..."

In the *Old Testament* of the *Bible*, many references are made to encircling dances, specifically those around wells. *Numbers XXI* contains the song of the well which begins "Spring up, o well. Sing ye unto it; to the well which the princes digged." The Semites mirrored the Hebrew veneration for wells, noting that they could receive or reject offerings like gems.

Decorating wells was predominant in Europe especially during May celebrations. During these celebrations tossing a coin or other "bribe" into the water was thought to appease the well spirit, which would thereby grant a wish. Some writers on this topic suggest that you come to a well alone at dawn or dusk after making a wish and toss in a rock. If you hear the echo of the rock splashing, the wish will come true.

It should be noted that wishing well customs have not been limited to wells and fountains, but are also seen in majestic locations like Niagara Falls.

Wheat

Hungarian farmers keep a sheath of wheat in the house every harvest as a wish for continued providence. They consider wheat the hope of the poor. This tradition is very similar in form to many harvest observances both in Europe and rural America that continued up through the turn of the century. In these, the last sheaf of corn or other grain was called "the maiden" and symbolized prosperity. To eat, bale, or throw away the maiden was akin to tossing away good luck.

Whitsunday

On the day after the traditional ascension of Christ, tongues of fire fell upon the faithful. The church celebrated this occasion with a flourish of festivities. One tradition was to go to a mountain just before sunrise. As the first rays of sun touched the horizon, one made a wish.

Willow

(see also *Trees*)

Two people who wish to strengthen their relationship may do so by following this old European procedure. Find a small willow sapling on the night of a waxing moon, and together tie a knot in one of its supple branches. As the tree grows strong, so too will your love. The knot binds the magic within, and the willow represents the flexibility necessary to maintaining a relationship.

For general wishes, tie the knot in any supple branch thanking the tree for its aid. When the wish manifests, release the knot.

Wind

Wind is a potent ally in wishing, providing a medium through which our physical representations of a wish may find movement. Examples here include feathers for joyful wishes, grain for improved finances, and flower petals for love.

Which wind you use in wishing will affect the outcome. A northern wind is best for calming influences and themes of rest or peace. Westerly winds deal with the emotions, any lunar or watery characteristics like insight, and improved flow. Eastern winds are for inception and hopefulness, being from the place of the rising sun. Finally, southerly winds bring power, purification, and energy.

To combine your wish symbol with the winds into a useful decoration, make wind chimes for yourself. Craft the chime out of appropriate woods, nuts, metals, or bells that will somehow intone your intention to the Universe. Then let the air do its magic!

Wine

(see also *Saki*)

In ancient times people poured out libations to the gods as an offering while they voiced their wishes. Wine was a sacred beverage to many ancient cultures, because fermentation was considered an act of the gods. In ancient Greece, pouring out wine invoked Bacchus' presence and blessings at any gathering.

Generally speaking, wine is a good component for wishes focused on company, hospitality, celebratory times, and abundance.

Wish boxes

(see also *Spell boxes*)

A slight variation on spell boxes as presented in Medici's *Good Magic*, wish boxes are made from paper or cardboard and decorated with special designs that represent the wish. The person making the wish should craft the box her/himself, if possible, to increase the personal energy in the finished token.

Once the box is decorated, fill it with a potpourri of flower petals and/or spices that also symbolize the goal. In the center of this sweet resting place, put a folded piece of paper the wish has been written clearly on. Close the box and wrap it with a string or ribbon. Place the wish box somewhere it will remain undisturbed. If you have an altar or sacred space in your home where it can accumulate more energy, all the better.

Once the wish is fulfilled, toss the wish box into a ritual fire with thankfulness, or give it to someone else who needs it. This way the positive magic that brought you good fortune likewise blesses others. Pass it on (see *Sayonara gift*)!

Witch hazel

This herb is known in Germany as *Zauber Strauch*, and the tree on which it grows is considered quite magical. Carve your wishes into its wood, or bury representations of them beneath the tree to grow.

Wreath (or crown)

Wear a wreath of an appropriate herb, wood, or flower while wishing to empower your magic. Early philosophers associated the head with the seat of God, and the circle with never-ending energy (i.e., eternity). Additionally, many civilizations used wreaths or crowns to acknowledge achievement.

In the Olympic games, a wreath of olive was worn by the winners. In the Isthmian games, it was a pine wreath, and in the Pythian games a beech wreath. In Greek marriage rituals, the brides wore a crown of parsley for happiness. The god Bacchus wore a circlet of ivy, and rulers wore crowns to denote their station. Wearing a similarly fashioned crown in your wishcraft encourages self-assurance in the magic.

Wood

(see also *Acorn, Apple, Ash leaf, Aspen, Beech, Buckthorn, Dogwood, Evergreen, Hazel, Rowan, Trees, Willow*)

Among the Norse, small slivers of wood were sometimes inscribed with runes to help bring magic to fruition. Similar items can be made for wishing and carved or painted with a symbol associated with your goal (see also *Symbols*). Once the wish comes true, ritually destroy this token with a grateful heart.

The Northern Europeans believed the best time to harvest wood for magic was at sunrise, noon, or sunset (see *Astrology, Dawn, Days*). The wood should always be cut from the direction that best represents your goal (i.e., west—healing/intuition; north—foundations/grounding; east—new beginnings/inception; south—energy/purification). Once the wood is cut, it should not touch the ground or the energy may drain out. Also, don't forget to thank the tree in some manner for its gift.

Words

(see also *Speaking in unison*)

In many stories and histories, specific words and phrases have been used for creating magic results. *Abracadabra, open sesame,* and *hocus pocus* are a few examples. While today these phrases have lost their potency because of stage magic, using spoken language is still an important part of wish making (see also *Stars*).

For example, when two people speak in unison, they should pinch each other or touch pinkies and make a wish (see *Speaking*). Victorians also believed if you say "rabbit" as your last word before going to sleep then "hare" upon rising, you will receive a gift or have a wish fulfilled within a month.

For more information on word power in wishing, return to the section beginning on page 24.

Yams

In Nigeria, yams are likened to deities. To find one growing randomly is regarded as most serendipitous.

In the West Indies, the word yam translates, "to eat," so this particular food might also be utilized for wishes of providence. Astrologically yams are ruled by Venus, making them also appropriate in matters of love.

Yarrow

In China, if you see a yarrow plant showing its first bud, you should make a wish. Yarrow is an honored plant there, revered for its abundance. It was the yarrow plant that gave birth to the I-Ching system of divination.

Yule

(see also *Christmas*)

In Bulgaria, the ancient God of Winter is the bearer of gifts at Yule. As the head of the house strikes the Yule log, and sparks appear, a wish must be made for luck (see Hutchinson and Adams in the bibliography).

In some Swedish homes, the matron of a house lights an angel candle during Yule celebrations while making a wish for the family. The flame of the candle causes a chime to ring, which sends the wish to heaven.

In Britain, special crackers are prepared for Yule. These are small crisp tubes, decorated with ribbons and paper, in which wishes for the new year are placed (not unlike Chinese fortune cookies). On Yule morning, everyone in the family takes one cookie and breaks it "open" to release the good luck and wishes within.

Listing of Deities

You may want Divine assistance in your wish's fulfillment. If so, it is important to know the Beings you are calling on, and how best to honor them in your sacred space. You need to say the names of the god or goddesses correctly, understand their characteristics, and cultivate an attitude of reverence in yourself before making any requests.

This list represents a small number of the world's deities from various points in history. If you are not comfortable with any of these, and are interested in researching further, please review the texts listed under "Gods and Goddesses" in the topical bibliography for more options.

Addad (Babylonian)

The god of foresight and the future, his holy symbols include lightning bolts and bulls. Call upon this being to help untangle fate's web. One caution exists, however. Addad also is a storm god whose transformations may not be gentle.

Adonai Aretz (Cabalistic)

A sacred name for God, in the 10th Sephirah, whose dominion is that of manifestation through will into the material plane. This effectively describes any type of spellcraft. To encourage this presence or assistance, burn yellow candles and oak-based incense. Add ivy, rock crystal, and willow branches to the sacred space. Stand in the center of an equal-armed cross when casting your wish.

Agni (India)

This being mediates between the gods and humankind, bearing our wishes and needs to their ears. He is also the god of hope and new beginnings. Honor Agni with any type of fire source, especially a torch, and/or a fan.

Aeolus (Greek)

The keeper of the winds, which he could not always control. When working with any of the four winds in your wishcraft, call on either Aeolus or the wind by its proper name. Boreas is the north wind, Zephyrus the west, Notos the south, and Eurus the east.

Aeons (Gnostic)

The embodiment of power, the origination of all things, and manifest thought. Sacred numbers are 8 and 22. Also effective in wishes focused on obtaining the truth in any situation.

Anat (Phoenicia)

This goddess's name means "holy one." She was so powerful that the other gods granted whatever Anat wished. To honor her in your wishing, don purple and burn coriander incense.

Angerona (Rome)

A deity whose dominion is silence and secrecy. Her festival day is December 21st.

Agizan (Voodoo)

Goddess who is humankind's psychic center and source. Honor her presence in your sacred space with a palm leaf. Agizan may be called upon for wishes of protection too.

Anu (Mesopotamian)

The Father God who presides over the fate of everything, even that of the Universe. Sacred emblems for Anu include the star and staff.

Aphrodite (Greek)

This goddess governs matters of love, creativity, generosity, and renewal. To call upon her, decorate your altar with sea shells, poppy, rose, and a whole pomegranate. Burn frankincense and myrrh. Corresponds with Venus in Rome.

Apollo (Greek and Roman)

A greater god who presides over spiritual goals that are accomplished through any art, including wishcraft. Honor this deity by burning bay incense and placing spring water on the altar.

Arianrhod (Wales)

The goddess of time, the stars, fertility and karma. Call upon her during a full moon. Her sacred symbol is a silver wheel.

Artemis (Greek)

The mistress of magical arts, Artemis will often swiftly intercede on behalf of her worshipers in many matters. To contact her, perform your wish spell on the 6th day after the new moon, and burn juniper wood in the sacred space.

Asa (Africa)

A god of mercy and help, useful in overcoming things that seem impossible.

Ashtart (Phoenician)

Goddess of the planet Venus who is also called the "guiding star," this Lady has an eight-pointed star and meteorites as emblems. Consider calling on Ashtart when wishing on stars or falling stars to empower the magic.

Amitabha (Tibet)

God of boundless light and salvation who offers aid when you feel as if your wishcraft is failing. Bring any red object into your sacred space when calling on this deity.

Amoghasiddhi (Tibet)

The god of perfect accomplishment whose sacred color is green.

Ba'ahth (Canaan)

As a greater goddess of trees and wells, Ba'ahth is good to invoke when working with either one of these wishing traditions.

Badb (Irish)

Goddess of wisdom and enlightenment, best suited for wishes focused on spiritual matters. Honor Badb in your craft with a cauldron full of boiling water or a crow's feather.

Banana Maiden (Celebes)

The goddess of transition and change, welcome her in your sacred space with the fruit which bears her name.

Benten (Japan)

A goddess of luck, wealth, love, and music, Benten carries a jewel that grants desires. Her symbols are a guitar, dragon, snake, salt water, and sword, and her festival is New Year. In Japan, people carry images of this goddess as a charm for accomplishment.

Bes (Egypt)

A god of luck and fortune, this divine figure was featured on amulets, charms, and talismans to help bring the bearer's wishes into reality. Bes is fond of mirrors, perfumes, and uplifting music, and is the god associated with dance and women's adornment.

Bragi (Norse)

A god of wit, cunning, and effective communication, including verbal magical formulas. To encourage Bragi's presence, play inspiring songs and pour out an offering of mead.

Brigit (Ireland/Wales)

The goddess of witchcraft and the occult, invoke her aid with poetic refrains recited near a fire source. Her sacred number is 19. Brigit is useful in wishes pertaining to prophesy, inspiration, and domestic issues.

Chuku (Africa)

A creative, helpful god. Honor his presence with ale or by communing in groves.

Circe (Greek)

The weaver of destiny, this goddess created and destroyed with knots bound and released in her hair. An excellent deity for knot wishcraft. Appropriate offerings for Circe include honey, fruit, and willow wood. Beware, however, as Circe does have a darker side. Do not invoke her when you feel gloomy, angry, or otherwise ill-disposed.

Dactyls (Greece)

Spirits who formed from the fingerprints of Rhea, these beings invented magical formulae. Call upon them when you're having trouble constructing your wishcraft effectively.

Dazhbog (Slavic)

God of happiness, fairness, just rewards, and destiny, his colors are yellow and gold.

Demeter (Greece)

A nature goddess who also governs magical philosophy, fidelity, renewal, matters of law, motherhood, and love. Her sacred symbols include rich soil and grain, both of which can become a component in your wishing, especially for growth or providence.

Donn (Ireland/Wales)

The goddess of the creative abyss and elemental control. Invoke her blessings using eloquent verbal entreaties.

Ea (Babylonian and Mesopotamian)

An all-purpose wishing deity who rules over incantations, magic, foresight, wisdom, and the greater mysteries. Especially useful to people who feel empowered by the water element.

Elohim (Cabalistic)

One of the great names for God, this name corresponds to the third Sephirah of the Tree of Life, governing one's personal faith. To encourage the blessings of Elohim on your spell, cover the altar in grey and pink cloth, burn a mixture of myrrh and thyme, and decorate the ritual space with lotus flowers and containers of water.

Erh-lang (China)

A shape-shifting god who both sustains and restores. His sacred number is 72.

Euphrosyne (Greek)

One of the three Graces who creates joy and gladness. Call upon this being to aid in wishes that have strong emotional import.

Faunus (Rome)

The life force of the world, from which we draw our energy for magic. To invoke this presence, perform your wish spell on February 15 in a natural setting with orchard fruits as an offering.

Fortuna (Rome)

A goddess whose domain is that of fate and chance. Have a wheel or cornucopia as you call on this being.

Freyja (Norse)

The goddess of luck, magic, cleverness, destiny, and foresight. Invoke her assistance on Friday the 13th by reciting poems in her honor or with an offering of flowers.

Fu-Hsing (China)

The god of happy destinies, his sacred animal is a bat.

Gabriel (Cabalistic)

Archangel of the ninth Sephirah, Gabriel presides over change, transformation, and divinatory insight. Since all wishcraft focuses on the desire to make specific alterations, Gabriel's assistance is most valuable. To honor him in your work, place silver candles on the alter, burn jasmine or violet incense, and decorate the area with lily petals. Rituals invoking Gabriel can be further empowered by working beneath a moon-lit sky.

Ganesha (India)

An elephant god who removes obstacles, also the god of luck and success. When one worships Ganesha in his festivals, he will fulfill wishes. Rice and flowers are traditional offerings.

Gibil (Assyria)

Call upon this god to intercede for you, especially in wishes pertaining to justice.

Gwydion (Wales)

Wizard and bard, and god of change. Honor him in your sacred space with music, fresh, flowing air, or the image of a white horse. (An alternative god from this tradition for similar goals is Taliesin, who was also a shape shifter.)

Hachiman (Japan)

A historical figure elevated to the status of the god of bravery and honor. He grants success in personal matters.

Haniel (Cabalistic)

Archangel of the seventh Sephirah, presiding over matters of creativity and inspiration, both important in personally meaningful wishing. Haniel may be drawn into your work by using yellow candles, burning rose-sandalwood incense, and decorating the sacred space with violet petals. Additionally, this being reacts positively to any place of beauty, natural settings being preferable.

Hecate (Greece)

The patroness of witches, charms, and spellcraft, this goddess is represented by a key or cauldron. Bathe yourself in henna before invoking her, and perform the wish ritual by torchlight for best results.

Heimdall (Norse)

God of the rainbow, keen vision and hearing, beginnings and protection. The ninth day of any month is a fitting time to request aid from this divinity. Have water in the sacred space and, if possible, work your wishcraft beneath a shining moon in a phase that is appropriate to your goal.

Hephaestus (Greek)

Another creative magical figure, Hephaestus was the metal and gem magician to the gods. Invoke him whenever working with gem- or metal-based wish spells. Forging tools or iron are appropriate in the sacred space for this deity.

Hermes (Greek)

When you need wishes to manifest quickly, turn to the feather-heeled messenger of the gods. Hermes has dominion over hermetic, elemental, and seasonally based wishcraft. Comparable to Mercury in Rome.

Horus (Egypt)

Call on Horus when you need creative problem-solving energies in your wishing. This being is often pictured as falcon-headed, perhaps representing insight. Horus' eyes are considered to be the sun and the moon, two objects strongly associated with wishing.

Innua (Eskimo)

The Great Spirit that exists in all things. Honor this being with sunlight or fresh air.

Iris (Greece)

The embodiment of the rainbow, this goddess carries your messages directly to the gods' ears. Honor her in your sacred space with figs and wheat-honey cakes.

Ishtar (Mesopotamian, Babylonian, Arabian)

A goddess with many names and attributes including life, order, lunar energy, oracles, and vision, all of which have application in wishcraft. An eight-pointed star, a dove, and a doubled-headed ax are among Ishtar's holy symbols. To honor her in your sacred space, cover the altar with a rainbow-colored cloth, and place a lapis on it.

Janus (Rome)

The god of good beginnings and navigation. Let him guide your wish to its best possible outcome. Honor him in the sacred space with two-sided items (like a two-headed coin), or cast your wish on New Year's Day for best success.

Kamrusepas (Hittite)

General goddess of spells and the art magic.

Khamael (Cabalistic)

The Archangels of the fifth Sephirah who governs will power and energy, two things indispensable in magic. All spells work through the will. To draw this power, place red cloth upon the altar, burn tarragon and basil, and decorate the sacred space with a pentagram made of fallen oak branches. Stand in the center of the pentagram when making your request, as this represents the meeting place of the elements, personal will, and the Sacred.

Khensu (Egypt)

This divine being's name literally means the "navigator." Release your wishes to him when you feel they need divine direction and guidance. Additionally, Khensu is an excellent figure for wishes of health and recuperation. His symbol is the crescent moon.

Khephera (Egypt)

A form of Ra who embodies the rising sun, this god's dominion is that of transformation, new beginnings, and miracles. His name literally means "he who becomes," and Khephera's symbol is the scarab. Greet this being at dawn for best results.

Kronos (Greek)

The father of time and inventor of magic. A good image to invoke when time is of the essence. Use sand or an hourglass to invoke and welcome this deity.

Kwan Yin (China)

A goddess of mercy who answers the prayers of her worshipers faithfully. She is especially receptive to women.

Lado (Slavic)

God of joy and well-being. Invoke his aid between the dates of May 25th and June 25th, and have water in the sacred space.

Lakshmi (India)

The goddess of success, victory, fate, and fortune, call upon her during the month of September using sacred dance as an invocation.

Lama (Sumerian)

A goddess who guides worshipers to the gods they invoke. Lama will intercede on your behalf with any deity in the Sumerian pantheon.

Lha (Tibet)

Types of guardian angels who aid and protect.

Lud (Ireland/Wales)

God of incantations, magic, healing, and wealth, welcome him to your rituals or spells by having a gold fish, a solar symbol, in the sacred space. Alternatively, any wooden items that are hand-made also please this being.

Lu-Hsing (China)

God of salaries, employment, and overall success, especially for financial wishes. His sacred animal is a deer.

Mananan (Ireland)

Son of the Irish Sea God, Lir, Mananan has a magical boat that is steered by the wishes of the occupant, over land or sea. This personification is also associated with Charon, and is an excellent figure for wishes pertaining to travel and protection.

Nabu (Mesopotamian)

A god who writes on the tablets of destiny. Call upon Nabu in wishes where your fate needs changing or assistance. Place writing implements in your sacred space to honor this god.

Nut (Egypt)

The personification of the stars, upon which we so often wish, Nut is known as the "life giver." Allow her to give life to your dreams. Her symbols are the cow or a round vase.

Odin (Norse)

The great, all-seeing father who presides over words of power, fate, magic, divination, and prophesy. Odin is pleased by written poetry, rain water, and freshly harvested items.

Ogun (Africa)

A god who removes obstacles and smoothes the way for your wish's manifestation. Have pieces of iron in the sacred space, and burn a snippet of your hair to honor him. Ogun is also the protective spirit of barbers.

Okuninushi (Japan)

A god of self-realization, he holds dominion over sorcery and cunning. Honor him in the sacred space with rich soil.

Ormazd (Persia)

The great god of Universal law and virtue. Welcome this being into your sacred space through the use of light (natural or candles). An excellent figure to call upon to make sure your wishcraft works for the greatest good.

Persephone (Greek)

The goddess who will help you overcome obstacles that impede your wishes, hopes, and dreams. Welcome her in your spell with corn, willow, pomegranate seeds, or narcissus flowers. Her name is Prosperina in the Roman pantheon.

Ra (Egypt)

The great creator god of the Egyptians, Ra controls magical spells. He is best invoked at noon, when the sun is at its height.

Ratziel (Cabalistic)

The Archangel associated with the second Sephirah and creative, manifesting energy. To invoke the assistance of this being in your wishing, use a blue altar cover, burn musk mixed with beechwood shavings, and place amaranth flowers and large stones in a circle around the sacred space.

Rin Po Che (Tibetan)

The great, accomplished magician whose flower is the lotus.

Sarasvati (India)

The motivational energy of the cosmos. Honor her beneath a crescent moon with lotus incense or flowers.

Selene (Greek)

An aspect of the moon who oversees all magic and spellcraft. When invoking, adorn your working space with hues of silver and gold, representing the will and the intuition working in harmony.

Shichi Kukujin (Japan)

The seven gods of happiness, governing the realms of prosperity, work, love, joy, longevity, luck, and bliss.

Shui-Khan (China)

A god who protects you from negative influences that can hinder your wishes. Also the god of forgiveness and inspiration. Honor him in the sacred space with rice cakes or turtle images.

Sin (Babylonian)

If you feel your wishcraft has been impeded by negative energy or ill-wishers, Sin is an excellent god to call upon for aid. He is the enemy of evil-doers, rules over the calendar, and is the god of destiny. His symbols include a full lunar sphere and lapis stone.

Thoth (Egypt)

The great Magus of Egyptian mythos, Thoth presides over all matters of ritual and spellcraft. To honor him, have honey and figs in the sacred space and work beneath a moon-lit sky.

Varuna (India)

A god ruling over the creative force and will necessary for wishcraft and cosmic order. Invoke him in the western quarter of the circle using water as an offering.

Zeus (Greek)

The god who grants heart's desires and improves luck! Encourage Zeus' blessings with oak-based incense and a cauldron filled with rain water. Corresponds with the Roman figure of Jupiter.

Appendix
Topical Bibliography

Folklore/Superstition/Myth

A World of Luck. Alexandria, VA: Time Life Books, 1991.

Alexander, Marc. *British Folklore*. New York, NY: Crescent Books, 1982.

Attenborough, David. *Journeys to the Past*. England: Lutterworth Press, 1981.

(author). "The Materials of Folklore." Journal of American Folklore 66 (1953): 70.

(author). "Folklore and Anthropology." Journal of American Folklore 66 (1953): 283.

Baker, Margaret. *Folklore and Customs of Rural England*. Totawa, NJ: Rowman & Littlefield, 1974.

Blecher, George and Lone Thygesen, eds. *Swedish Folktales and Legends*. NY: Pantheon Books, 1993.

Boland, Margaret. *Old Wives Lore for Gardeners*. Farrar, Straus & Giroux, NY: 1976.

Budge, E. A. Wallis. *Amulets and Talismans*. New Hyde Park, NY: University Books, 1968.

Cavendish, Richard, ed. *Man, Myth and Magic*. London, England: Purnell, 1972.

Chapman, Colin. *Shadows of the Supernatural*. IL: Lion Publishing, 1990.

Chaundler, Christine. *Book of Superstitions*. NJ: Citadel Press, 1970.

Complete Book of Fortune. New York, NY: Crescent Books, 1936.

Cooper, J. C. *Symbolic and Mythological Animals*. Hammersmith, England: Aquarian Press, 1992.

Cunningham, Scott. *The Magic in Food*. St. Paul, MN: Llewellyn Publications, 1991.

Dundes, A. *Study of Folklore*. Englewood Cliffs, NJ: Prentice Hall, 1965.

Felding, William J. *Strange Superstitions and Magical Practices*. New York, NY: Paperback Library, 1968.

Gonzalez-Wippler, Migene. *Amulets and Talismans*. St. Paul, MN: Llewellyn Publications, 1995.

Graves, Robert. *The Greek Myths*. England: Penguin Publishing, 1983.

Hand, Wayland D. *Popular Beliefs and Superstitions*. Boston, MA: K. Hall, 1981.

Hendricks, Rhoda. *Mythologies of the World*. NY: McGraw Hill, 1979.

Kunz, G. Frederick. *Curious Lore of Precious Stones*. NY: Dover Publications, 1913.

Leach, Maria, ed. *Standard Dictionary of Folklore, Mythology and Legend*. NY: Funk & Wagnall, 1972.

Loewe, Michael, ed. *Oracles and Divination*. Boulder CO: Shambhala Publishing, 1981.

Lorrie, Peter. *Superstition*. UK: Labyrinth Publishing, 1992.

McAlpine, Helen and William. *Japanese Tales and Legends*. NY: Oxford University Press, 1958.

Maple, Eric. *Superstitions and the Superstitious*. CA: Wilshire Books, 1973.

New Larousse Encyclopedia of Mythology. Hong Kong: Prometheus Press, 1959.

Quaint Customs and Manners in Japan. Tokyo: Mock Joya, (no date).

Opie, Iona, and Tatem, Moira, eds. *Dictionary of Superstition*. NY: Oxford Publishing, 1989.

Pennick, Nigel. *Magic in the Northern Tradition*. England: Aquarian Press, 1989.

Potter, Carole. *Knock on Wood*. New York: Beaufort Books, Inc., 1983.

Scott, Rev. J. Loughran. *Bulfinch's Age of Fable*. Philadelphia PA: David McKay, 1898.

Telesco, Patricia. *Folkways*. St. Paul, MN: Llewellyn Publications, 1995.

Tuleja, Tad. *Curious Customs*. NY: Harmony Books, 1987.

Wootton A. *Animal Folklore, Myth and Legend*. NY: Blanford Press, 1986.

Food and Beverage Lore

Arnold, John P. *Origin and History of Beer and Brewing*. Chicago, IL: Wahl-Henius Institute of Fermentology, 1911.

Chase, A. W., MD. *Receipt Book and Household Physician*. Detroit, MI: F. B. Dickerson Company, 1908.

Cunningham, Scott. *The Magic in Food*. St. Paul, MN: Llewellyn Publications, 1991.

Harlan, William. *Illustrated History of Eating and Drinking through the Ages*. NY: American Heritage Publishers, 1968.

MacNicol, Mary. *Flower Cookery*. NY: Fleet Press, 1967.

Spayde, John. *Japanese Cooking*. NJ: Chartwell Books, 1984.

Stafford, Edward Lord. *The Form of Curry*. London, England: J. Nichols Co., 1780.

Tannahill, Reay. *Food in History*. New York, NY: Stein & Day, 1973.

Telesco, Patricia. *Kitchen Witch's Cookbook*. St. Paul MN: Llewellyn Publications, 1994.

_____. *Witch's Brew*. St. Paul, MN: Llewellyn Publications, 1994.

Gods and Goddesses

Carlyon, Richard. *A Guide to the Gods*. London, England: Heinemann/Quixote, 1981.

Conway, D. J. *Ancient and Shining Ones*. St. Paul, MN: Llewellyn Publications, 1993.

Farrar, Janet and Stewart. *The Witches' God*. Custer WA: Phoenix Publishing, 1989.

_____. *The Witches' Goddess*. Custer WA: Phoenix Publishing, 1987.

Hendricks, Rhoda. *Mythologies of the World*. NY: McGraw Hill, 1979.

Monaghan, Patricia. *The Book of Goddesses and Heroines*. St. Paul MN: Llewellyn Publications, 1981.

Scott, Rev. J. Loughran. *Bulfinch's Age of Fable*. Philadelphia PA: David McKay, 1898.

Herbs, Plants, Flowers, and Stones

Beyerl, Paul. *Master Book of Herbalism*. Custer, WA: Phoenix Publishing, 1984.

Black, William George. *Folk Medicine*. NY: Burt Franklin Company, 1883, 1970.

Budge, E. A. Wallis. *Amulets and Superstitions*. NY: Dover Publications, 1930.

Budge, E. A. Wallis. *Amulets and Talismans*. London, England: Oxford University Press, 1930.

Chase, A. W., MD. *Receipt Book and Household Physician*. Detroit MI: F. B. Dickerson Company, 1908.

Clarkson, Rosetta. *Green Enchantment*. New York, NY: Macmillan Publishing, 1940.

Culpepper, Nicholas. *Complete Herbal and English Physician*. Glenwood IL: Meyerbooks, 1991. Originally published 1841.

Cunningham, Scott. *Encyclopedia of Crystal, Gem and Metal Magic*. St. Paul, MN: Llewellyn Publications, 1995.

Cunningham, Scott. *Encyclopedia of Magical Herbs*. St. Paul, MN: Llewellyn Publications, 1988.

Cunningham, Scott. *The Magic in Food*. St. Paul, MN: Llewellyn Publications, 1991.

Fox, William, MD. *Family Botanic Guide*, 18th edition. Sheffield England: William Fox & Sons, 1907.

Gordon, Leslie. *Green Magic*. NY: Viking Press, 1977.

Gregor, Arthur S. *Amulets, Talismans and Fetishes*. NY: Scribner's, 1975.

Keller, M. S. *Mysterious Herbs and Roots*. Culver City, CA: Culver City Press, 1978.

Kunz, G. Frederick. *Curious Lore of Precious Stones*. NY: Dover Publications, 1913.

Palaiseul, Jean. *Grandmother's Secrets*. NY: G. P. Putnam's Sons, 1974.

Riotte, Louise. *Sleeping with a Sunflower*. Pownal, VT: Garden Way Publishing, 1987.

Rodale's Complete Illustrated Encyclopedia of Herbs. Emmaus, PA: Rodale Publishing, 1987.

Skinner, Charles M. *Myths and Legends of Flowers, Trees, Fruits and Plants*. Philadelphia, PA: Lippincott, 1925.

Williams, Judith. *Jude's Home Herbal*. St. Paul, MN: Llewellyn Publications, 1992.

History (General)

Aero, Rita. *Things Chinese*. Garden City, NY: Dolphin Press, 1980.

Attenborough, David. *Journeys to the Past*. England: Lutterworth Press, 1981.

Becker, H., and Barnes, H. E. *Social Thought from Lore to Science*. NY: Dover Publications, 1960.

Broth, Patricia and Don. *Food in Antiquity*. Frederick A. Praeger, NY: 1969.

Brown, Peter. *The World of Late Antiquity*. London: Thames & Hudson, 1971.

Day, Cyrus Lawrence. *Quipus and Witches' Knots*. KS: University of Kansas Press, 1967.

Everyday Life Through the Ages. London, England: Reader's Digest Association Limited, 1992.

Hearn, Lafcadio. *Japan*. London, England: Macmillan, 1905.

Magnall, Richmal. *Historical and Miscellaneous Questions*. London, England: Longman, Brown, Green & Longman, 1850.

Holidays, Festivals, and Celebrations

Bauer, Helen. *Japanese Festivals*. NY: Doubleday, 1968.

Budapest, Z. E. *Grandmother of Time*. New York: Harper & Row Publishing, 1989.

Hutchison, Ruth, and Adams, Ruth. *Every Day's a Holiday*. NY: Harper & Brothers Publishers, 1951.

Ickis, Marguerite. *Book of Festival Holidays*. New York: Dodd, Mead & Co., 1964.

Murray, Keith. *Ancient Rites and Ceremonies*. Toronto, Canada: Tudor Press, 1980.

Mystical Year. Mysteries of the Unknown Series. Alexandria, VA: Time-Life Books, 1992.

Spicer, Dorothy Gladys. *The Book of Festivals*. NY: Woman's Press, 1937.

Telesco, Patricia. *Folkways*. St. Paul MN: Llewellyn Publications, 1995.

_____. *Seasons of the Sun*. York Beach, ME: Samuel Weiser, 1996.

_____. *Urban Pagan*. St. Paul, MN: Llewellyn Publications, 1993

Van Straalen, Alice. *The Book of Holidays Around the World*. NY: E. P. Dutton, 1986.

Magic/Magical History

Ancient Wisdom and Secret Sects. Mysteries of the Unknown Series. Alexandria, VA: Time-Life Books, 1989.

Banis, Victor. *Charms, Spells and Curses for the Millions*. Los Angeles: Sherbourne Press, 1970.

Browne, Lewis. *The Believing World*. New York: Macmillan Company, 1959.

Cavendish, Richard. *History of Magic*. NY: Taplinger Publishing, 1977.

Cavendish, Richard, ed. *Man, Myth and Magic*. London: Purnell, 1972.

Crowley, Brian and Esther. *Words of Power*. St. Paul, MN: Llewellyn Publications, 1991.

Cunningham, Scott. *Art of Divination*. CA: The Crossing Press, 1993

Drury, Nevill. *Dictionary of Mysticism and the Occult*. New York, NY: Harper and Row, 1985.

Farrar, Janet and Stewart. *Spells and How They Work*. Custer, WA: Phoenix Publishing, 1990.

Finley, J. *Sorcery*. Boston MA: Routledge & Kegan, 1985.

Froud, Brian and Alan Lee. *Fairies*. England: Souvenir Press, 1978.

Guiley, Rosemary Ellen. *Witches and WitchCraft*. New York, NY: Facts on File, Inc., 1989

Hall, Manly. *Secret Teachings of All Ages*. Los Angeles CA: Philosophical Research Society, 1977.

Kieckhefer, Richard. *Magic in the Middle Ages*. MA: Cambridge University Press, 1989.

Matthews, John, ed. *World Atlas of Divination*. Bullfinch Press, 1992.

Murray, Keith. *Ancient Rites and Ceremonies*. Toronto, Canada: Tudor Press, 1980.

Pennick, Nigel. *Magic in the Northern Tradition*. England: Aquarian Press, 1989.

Spence, Lewis. *Encyclopedia of the Occult*. London: Bracken Books, 1988.

Starhawk. *The Spiral Dance*. NY: Harper & Row, 1979.

Waite, A. E. *Occult Sciences: A Compendium of Transcendental Doctrine and Experiment*. Kila, MT: Kessinger Publishing Company, 1993 (reprint).

Zolar. *Encyclopedia of Ancient and Forbidden Knowledge*. CA: Nash Publications, 1970.

Miscellaneous:

Oesterley, W. O. E. *The Sacred Dance*. Brooklyn, NY: Dance Horizons; MA: Cambridge University Press, 1923.

Walker, Barbara. *Women's Dictionary of Symbols and Sacred Objects*. San Francisco, CA: Harper Row Publishing, 1988.

Webster's New World Dictionary. Englewood Cliffs, NJ: Prentice Hall, 1979.

Webster's Universal Unabridged Dictionary. NY: World Syndicate Publishing, 1937.

BOOKS BY THE CROSSING PRESS

An Astrological Herbal for Women

By Elisabeth Brooke

An extensive guide to the use of herbs in healing the mind, body and spirit, organized by planetary influence. Includes the astrological significance of 38 common herbs, as well as their physical, emotional, and ritual uses.

$12.95 • Paper • ISBN 0-89594-740-41

Ariadnes's Thread: A Workbook of Goddess Magic

By Shekinah Mountainwater

"One of the finest books on women's spirituality available." —*Sagewoman*
"A very good, practical book ... recommended."   —*Library Journal*

$16.95 • Paper • ISBN 0-89594-475-8

Casting the Circle: A Women's Book of Ritual

By Diane Stein

A comprehensice guide including 23 full rituals for waxing, full, and waning moons, the eight Sabats, and rites of passage.

$14.95 • Paper • ISBN 0-89594-411-1

The Language of Dreams

By Patricia Telesco

Patricia Telesco outlines a creative, interactive approach to understanding the dream symbols of our inner life. Interpretations of more than 800 dream symbols incorporate multi-cultural elements with psychological, religious, folk, and historical meanings so the imagery of every entry speaks to a diverse range of individuals.

$16.95 • Paper • ISBN 0-89594-836-2

Shamanism as a Spiritual Practice for Daily Life

By Tom Cowan

This inspirational book blends elements of shamanism with inherited traditions and contemporary religious commitments.
"An inspiring spiritual call."   —*Booklist*

$16.95 • Paper • ISBN 0-89594-838-9

Spinning Spells, Weaving Wonders:
Modern Magic for Everyday Life

By Patricia Telesco

This essential book of over 300 spells tells how to work with simple, easy-to-find components and focus creative energy to meet daily challenges with awareness, confidence, and humor.

$14.95 • Paper • ISBN 0-89594-803-6

A Woman's I Ching

By Diane Stein

Finally, a feminist interpretation of the popular ancient text for divining the character of events. Stein's version reclaims the feminine, or yin, content of the ancient work and removes all oppressive language and imagery. Her interpretation envisions a healing world in which women can explore different roles free from the shadow of patriarchy.

$16.95 • Paper • ISBN 0-89594-857-5

The Wiccan Path: A Guide for the Solitary Practitioner

By Rae Beth

"Booksellers familiar with the popularity of Scott Cunningham's Solitary books should be aware that this work deserves equal, if not greater status. An absolute masterpiece of Wiccan lore."   *—New Age Retailer*

$12.95 • Paper • ISBN 0-89594-744-7

A Wisewoman's Guide to Spells, Rituals and Goddess Lore

This is a remarkable compendium of magical lore, psychic skills and women's mysteries.

$12.95 • Paper • ISBN 0-89594-779-X

To receive a current catalog from The Crossing Press,
please call toll-free,
800-777-1048.
Visit our Website on the Internet at: www.crossingpress.com